When The
Dust Settled

WHEN THE DUST SETTLED

JOE POTOSI

Xulon Press

The author currently resides in the Midwest with his wife and two sons. He has taken an active role in the lives of his children helping coach their teams and attending all of their activities. He is an Ordained Minister. He works for a small church and does outreach to college students. His ministry has impacted students from all over the world. His passion is to be a role model and mentor to young adults. He wants to teach others that with faith, determination and hard work they can overcome any obstacle in life. He knows from his own life experiences how positive or negative influences can impact a person, but the choices they make will determine the direction their life goes. Writing the stories in this book were difficult and the memories were pianful as he relived each one. The reward of putting the memories into words has allowed him to have forgiveness in his heart for the abuse, neglect, and the hatred spewed at him as a child. He feels that in writing his book he has gained insight into his past and found direction for his future.

This book contains what I went through as a child; it is what I remember and what I experienced. I have changed the names in this book to protect privacies.

Xulon Press
2301 Lucien Way #415
Maitland, FL 32751
407.339.4217
www.xulonpress.com

© 2017 by Joe Potosi

The cover is a painting; created by my sister Toots. It is a silhouette of me in the chaotic world in which I lived. In spite of everything, when the dust settled, I was still standing.

Edited by Xulon Press.

Scripture quotations taken from the New King James Version (NKJV). Copyright © 1982 by Thomas Nelson, Inc. Used by permission. All rights reserved.

Printed in the United States of America.

ISBN-13: 978-1-54561-297-2

This book is dedicated to the one person who was always there for me: *my hero, my sister "Toots"*.

FOREWORD

During one's lifetime, degrees of challenges and hardships can be expected; however, some individuals find themselves in hardships so dire, so desperate and inconceivable to the average person. This was the case for us: a poor family consisting of a mother struggling to raise six children (a daughter and five sons); living in mostly undesirable habitats experiences the author went through will give you pause, forcing you to ask how anyone can overcome such deficits. Only by the grace of God, through God's abundant mercy and grace, all things are possible in His perfect timing. Although we weren't aware of it at the time, our Heavenly Father was always there: watching over us, protecting us, preparing us for His will from which we can be transformed into something far better than where we'd begun. Really, difficulties can be gifts, helping to build character; a toughening that would serve us well during our lifetimes and allow us to rely on God for hope and healing.

Despite the many challenges, my brother always looked after us, protecting and mentoring us. My brother, my hero! He was a father figure and a role model to the rest of us four younger boys. He taught me about sports, how football and baseball were played, rules of the game. He taught me many things that a father would normally teach his son; wish I would have told him "thank you" more often. My brother represented strength, protection, *fairness and encouragement. Although we all had a challenging upbringing, his experiences were more far more challenging because he was the oldest of five boys; more was expected and required of him. He carried a heavier load of responsibilities, and his experiences were also harder because he had known what it was like to have a relationship with our father, and then be apart from it. He personifies the phrase "Defying the odds". Through his life story, you will see God's hand at work.*

As the title "When the Dust Settled" evokes an image of the calm after a storm, the stories in the pages of this book chronicle my older brother's perspective of these extreme hardships (social economic, environment, relational and other). It will take you on the real-life journey through the struggle to understand our places in the world, coping with and, ultimately, triumphing over these hardships. This is really a story of tenacity, resilience, introspection, redemption and forgiveness. As you delve into this real-life American odyssey, I hope you are inspired.

Thank you brother!

Love, Marty

ACKNOWLEDGMENTS

First of all, to my wife who has always supported, encouraged, and pushed me along on this journey. I love you more than life itself.

To my sons, the sparkle in my eyes! I thank God for you. I love you very much.

To my sister Toots, thank you for always being there for me. Even though you were facing problems of your own, you put my welfare before yours. You are the personification of what it means to be a hero inside and out. Thank you for the artwork that is the cover of this book. It is priceless to me.

To my brother Marty, thank you for taking this journey with me. Thank you for the wonderful foreword to this project. It is very heartfelt and moving. I love you.

To my brother Greg who suggested the title of this book many years before I had even decided to write it.

To my in-laws, thank you for accepting me from day one and loving me unconditionally.

1
HUMBLE BEGINNINGS

My earliest memories was when we lived on a second-floor apartment on Broadway and 7th Street in Rockford, Illinois. It was the summer of 1970. Rockford is a small city ninety miles Northwest of Chicago. Our apartment was a real dump. I don't know what was worse—the mice or the roaches. It was a two-bedroom with crappy electric. There were holes in the walls and appliances that had seen better days. The oven door fell off the hinges when opened too fast. The apartment was very drafty as well. In the winter months, it was a real challenge to stay warm. Often Toots and I slept with layers of clothes on. Despite how terrible the apartment was, Mom kept it spotless.

The neighborhood we lived in was near downtown. That was good because we didn't have a car. Whenever we needed anything, it was a short walk for my folks. My sister Toots was four. She had long, flowing brown hair and green eyes. She was so caring, nurturing, and loving toward me. She was the one person who was always by my side and the one person I could trust. I was three. I had brown hair and hazel eyes. I was quite chubby and klutzy.

Every Sunday, Mom made us a big breakfast. My favorite was pancakes. I think Mom made the best pancakes in the whole world, and we usually argued over who gets the last one. The problem was Toots liked pancakes, too—probably more than me.

As I prepared to dig into the pile of pancakes, Dad said grace.

"God, thank you for the food you provided for us. Thank you for our good health. Please help me to find a job. One last thing, God, thank you for another baby. Help us to be the best parents. Amen!" My jaw dropped. I looked over to Toots. She jumped up to her feet and started to jump up and down.

"Yeah! We are having another baby," Toots yelled. I couldn't hold back my excitement. I ran over to her to join in the celebration with Mom and Dad.

Dad was a very handsome man. He was five feet, nine inches with a muscular build. He had curly dark-brown hair, hazel eyes, and pearl white teeth—so handsome. He reminded me of James Dean, the movie star. He was much taller than Mom. She was four feet, eleven inches, with brown hair and green eyes. I looked on as the two of them embrace each other. Whenever we were in public, Dad's affection toward her never waned. Often, they walked hand-in-hand. Dad called Mom "June Bug." I didn't know what that means, but Mom seemed to like it. Dad was a big fan of the *Ed Sullivan Show*. Mom and Dad would sit on the couch snuggling together while Toots and I lay on the floor in front of the TV. When Dad wanted to entertain us, he liked to imitate Ed Sullivan. He was so funny I didn't think there was anything my dad could not do. They were so loving to Toots and me. Our parents were always directing hugs, kisses, and kind words toward us.

My folks had a friend who lived in the first-floor apartment. Mary was a heavy-set, single white mother with three children. Her son Dion had long, black hair and light-brown skin. He was five years old. He was a cool friend. However, he was always getting in trouble with his mom for one reason or another. Whether it was fighting with his sister or whatever, it seemed to me that Mary had a very short fuse toward him. I felt sorry for him. Stacy was four. She had green eyes and auburn-colored hair. She was not as outgoing as her brother. And there was Mary's infant daughter Zion. She was so adorable with a full head of black hair and brown eyes. Mom and Dad both found jobs. In need of a babysitter, Mom asked Mary if she would be willing to babysit us. Mary apparently did not work because she was always home. She agreed to the job, and before I knew it, Toots and I spent our days with her and her kids in the downstairs apartment. It was a very dirty place. Dirty clothes were everywhere in mountainous piles. And there was the faint smell of a combination of cigarettes, dirty diapers, and sour milk.

She seemed a little different. I did not know what it was about her, but Dad called her Crazy Mary. I was afraid to look at her eyes, which were crazy to me. They looked void of any compassion. On most evenings when the folks would return home, Mom, Dad, and Mary would sit around and drink booze. They would get real weird while drunk. In fact, Mary liked to challenge Dad to an arm-wrestling match. I watched on with my sister as Mary would beat him every time. I could not help but wonder if that was why Dad called her Crazy Mary. She had more strength than a man—more than just any man—but also my hero, my dad, and that really scared me.

I was scared because I saw how she would just go off the handle and beat her kids when they did something wrong. What if, while babysitting us, she went into a fit of rage toward me or Toots? Who would stop her? Mom was very pregnant now, and Dad acted like he was afraid of her.

Baby Marty

Thursday September 10, 1970, I was awakened out of a deep sleep. Dad was shaking me.

"Joey, Joey, wake up!' I could tell he is a nervous wreck.

"Joey, come into the kitchen. Hurry up!"

Still in a haze, I stumbled into the kitchen. It was 3:00 a.m. I saw Mom making her way down the stairs toward the front door. She was breathing heavy and struggling to walk.

I followed Mom and ask, "Where are you going, Mom?"

"Joey, we need to go to the hospital. I am going to have the baby." I was frozen in place, trying to comprehend what is taking place.

"How are you getting to the hospital, Mom?"

"I called a taxi," Dad blurted out as he rushed past me. By the time I reached the bottom of the stairs, Mary was motioning me into her apartment. I ignored her and followed Mom and Dad outside.

'Terry, where is the taxi!" Mom screamed.

"It should be here any moment, June," he says.

3

"Go into Mary's and call them again. The baby is almost here!"
She screamed. Dad ran back into the building. I was concerned for
Mom's welfare at that point. I could tell she was in a ton of pain.

"Mom, I am staying here until the taxi shows up."

Thank you, Joey," she managed to say through her pain.

Just as Dad reappeared with Toots, Mary, and her kids, the taxi
pulled up. The cabbie saw what was happening and jumped out
to help. Mary, Dad, and the taxi driver assisted Mom to the front
seat. Dad quickly closed her door and jumped into the back seat.
He looked like he was going to faint.

"Dad, are you okay?"

"You just go with Mary." Just as the cabbie prepared to pull off,
Mary hollered, "Don't worry, guys. I will take good care of your
kids." That was not very reassuring to me. I was really worried
about Mom. I have never seen her in pain like this before. Toots
looks up to me. I guess she could see the concern in my eyes.

"Everything is going to be okay, man. Before you know it, we
will be welcoming the newest addition into our family." As I looked
into her eyes, I could tell she was at ease about all of this. I instantly
felt relaxed. I won't worry."

"Okay, kids, let's get back into the apartment," Mary said as
she lead the way.

"Toots, you and Joey can sleep on the couch. Dion and Stacy,
get to bed!" I looked on as Mary took the baby and retreated to her
bedroom. Toots got comfortable on one end of the couch and was
sleeping within seconds. I finally drifted off to sleep. The next two
days were dreadful. We had not heard a word from Dad or Mom. I
was watching cartoons with all the kids when I heard a commotion
coming from the hallway. I jumped up and ran into the hallway.
There was Mom holding Marty. My baby brother was so beautiful.
I could not believe he was sleeping through all the racket. Dad
was standing behind Mom, looking down at Marty. Dad looked so
happy, smiling from ear to ear. Dad and Mary were taking turns
holding the baby. I wanted to hold him, too.

"Can I hold the baby, Mom?"

"You need to just wait until we get upstairs and settled in, honey"

"Okay," I responded. In short order, Dad led us up to the apartment. I could not wait to hold my little brother. I followed Mom around the apartment, just waiting for the chance.

"You guys go sit on the couch, so you can hold the baby." I ran as fast as I could, beating Toots to the couch. Mom handed Marty over to Toots first. She instructed us on how to hold the baby. Now it was my turn to hold the baby I didn't want to let him go. He was so wonderful.

Over time, Mom taught us how to help feed, bathe, and change the baby's diapers. Toots caught on to everything so easy. I struggled with everything. Especially changing diapers. It was cloth that was held on each side by a huge pin. That was the hardest part for me. To pin the diaper without sticking Marty took real skill.

On Friday morning, as we were enjoying family time around the breakfast table, Mom informed us.

"Your dad and I applied for low-income housing a couple of years ago, with the hope that we could get placed in a decent area. I got a letter in the mail yesterday. We have been accepted at Jane Addams, the new housing project near the health department!" I overheard Mom and Dad mention how they would love to live there.

"That is groovy, man" Toots said. I am happy, too.

"Do I get my own bedroom, Dad?" I ask.

"No, it is only a two bedroom, but everything is new. It will be so much better, son!" You don't have to sell me on it.

"Can we move now?" Toots blurted out.

"No, we have a move-in date for two weeks from now."

"Okay, cool," Toots and I said in unison.

"There is one more thing we want to tell you both," she said as she fed Marty.

'What is it? Are we getting a car?'

"No, Joey! I am having another baby" *This is way too much excitement for one day*, I thought.

Toots interjected, "If it's a girl, can I name her?"

"Sure, you can," Dad said, "We are so blessed. God has been so good to us."

5

Secretly, I was hoping we would be rid of Mary after the move. She was so angry and unpredictable. I thought perhaps Dad wanted to have her help with the heavy work. He was no fool.

December 26, 1970, was moving day. Toots and I were tasked with watching Marty in the apartment while Mom, Dad, and his friends loaded up the U-Haul. It was a real chore to get the couch and a few of the bigger items down the steep stairs leading to the street. Once they had everything loaded, Dad invited everyone up for a drink. One drink led to two, then three. Dad got drunk. Mom had been napping, unaware of the situation. When she woke up, I watched as she stormed into the living room right up to Dad.

"What the hell are you doing? Why are you drinking? You have to drive the U-Haul, you moron!"

"June, it's okay. I am fine. Let me finish this beer, and we can go."

"No, you are finished now," as she grabbed the can of beer and dumped it down the kitchen sink.

"June bug, Jimmy can drive the U-Haul if you are that concerned."

"No, he can't. It is in your name. If something happen with him behind the wheel, you will be in big trouble. Toots and Joey, get your coats on. Terry, you guys go get our bed taken apart and carried down to the truck." Now ready, I followed Mom downstairs and out to the U-Haul. She sat in the middle of the front seat with Marty on her lap. Toots jumped in next. We could hear Dad and the guys in the back of the truck, putting the last few items in place. Dad reappeared and jumped behind the wheel.

"Are we ready?" he asked as he started the truck.

"What do you think, idiot?" Mom barked at him.

"We been sitting in this cold truck for far too long. Let's go!" Just as Dad began to pull off, Mary jumped in front of the truck.

"Wait for me!" Dad slammed on the brakes just in time. It's obvious Mary is feeling good after throwing back a few beers with Dad.

"Crap," Mom mumbled.

"Let's go, Mary," Dad says. We watched as Mary opened the passenger door and crammed her kids onto the seat next to us.

"Mary, there is not enough room for all of you. Can't you see that?"

"Nonsense, June," she said as she proceeded to place Zion on one knee and Stacy on the other. She then put the baby on her lap.

"Okay. Let's go, Terry. We have a truck to unload." I was stuck right next to her. Her hideous red polyester pants were rubbing against my leg. I hoped that does not rub off on me.

Dad was acting nervous behind the wheel.

"Terry! You need to pay attention to the road! You almost side-swiped that car in the other lane, you moron!"

"Hey June! This is a big truck. I am doing my best. I drove trucks in the Army — relax!"

"I will relax when I am settled in the apartment." It didn't take very long to get to the new place.

Once we arrived at the apartment, the excitement of seeing the new place kicked in. Once I climbed out of the truck, I caught up to Mom, who was carrying Marty toward the apartment. As Mom turned the key and pushed open the door, I was shocked. I followed Mom into the apartment followed by Dad and Toots. I could not get over how big it was. I raced upstairs with Toots to see the bedrooms.

"The bedrooms are big, Toots"

"Yep, and I get to put my bed by the window." We went back downstairs to check out the rest of the apartment. Dad stopped us as we entered the living room.

"You guys need to go outside and help with unloading the truck," Dad said.

Toots lead the way back out to the U-Haul. I noticed a black boy and girl watching us unload the truck. I saw them when we first arrived, but I did not think much of it at the time.

Later that afternoon, Dad kept his word to his friends by providing beer to all those who helped move. Mary has never been bashful about anything, especially when it came to drinking booze. Dad was having a drunkfest in the kitchen while Toots and I were helping Mom unpack boxes in the living room. I could tell she was upset that he was drinking instead of helping us. It wasn't like there was not anything to do, after all. Mom threw down an empty box in frustration and stormed into the kitchen.

"Okay, that's it. The party is over. Thanks for all of your help, but you need to go now." Just then there was a knock on the door. I watched as Mom hustled to answer it.

"Hi guys! Can I help you?" I could see it was the kids I saw before.

"Hi, my name is Lisa, and this is my brother Barry."

"Nice to meet you, honey; come inside." Mom walked the kids up the three stairs just inside the front door just as Dad took his drunken friends outside. She walked the kids into the living room where we were working. Toots walked up to Lisa.

"Hi, my name is Toots. What is your name?"

"I am Lisa. How old are you?"

"I am four," Toots said.

"Oh, so am I. Do you want to play later?"

"Yeah, if it's okay with Mom." I built up the courage to talk to the boy. He was a lot bigger and taller than me. He had a dark-brown complexion and short hair. He looked very intimidating.

"Hey, I am Joey. Who are you?"

"My name is Barry."

"Okay, do you live around here?"

"Yeah, I live right across from you on the corner."

"Alright, cool."

"I will be going to the rec center in a day or two. If you want to go with me, you can meet some of the other kids."

"Okay, I don't know where it is. Can you come by when you go there?"

"I will stop back, Joey. See you," he said as he shook my hand. I walked him to the front door. Things are already looking up in the new neighborhood. The only kids I really hung around were Mary's children. It will be nice to become friends with older kids for sure.

Over the next several weeks, I made a bunch of new friends. I was so content to be in the new apartment, but things were not well on the home front.

Mary and Mom's other friends were at the house a lot, they would stay late almost every night. I noticed Mom was drinking more and more, and Dad didn't seem happy with her choices. I woke up to them arguing in the kitchen every morning. It was times like these that I would find myself wanting to go play with my friend Barry. He was my very first true friend. I felt safe with him. I mean, when Mom had her little get-togethers with friends while Dad was away, I didn't feel safe around her. She would get drunk and very mean toward Toots and me. I have never seen this side of her. Was it because of the new people she had spent all her time with or is it something else?

From time to time, Dad and Mom would have people over on Sundays to play cards. Most of the people who came were folks from the neighborhood. One guy that would come over every week was Tyrone. He was a big black man who stood six feet, five inches, and very heavy. He looked to be around 300 pounds. Dad looked so puny next to him. I didn't know who was crazier—him or Mary. She was here all the time with her kids. She drank booze like a man. The four of them would sit and drink until late into the night until they were all good and drunk. Toots and I fended for ourselves and looked after Marty, which was becoming an all too often an occurrence.

In my mind I thought the love that Dad and Mom had for each other would grow, but instead they continued to drift apart. With my Mom being pregnant, Toots and I tried to help as much as possible around the house. As time went on, we saw less and less of Dad and more of this guy Tyrone. I didn't know where Dad was all this time, but I missed him. I wanted him home.

Toots and I woke up early on Saturday morning. We raced downstairs to watch cartoons. I loved the smell of coffee that was coming from the kitchen. I walked into the kitchen to greet Mom. I saw her standing over the kitchen sink hollering into the phone. Click. She slammed the phone down onto the base on the wall, and returned to her cigarette and coffee.

"Toots," Mom said, "Go get Marty and bring him down for breakfast."

"Can I do it, Mom?" I asked.

"Yeah, go ahead"

I ran up the stairs and grabbed Marty from his crib. I could smell that he pooped in his diaper. I carried Marty down to where Toots was in the living room watching cartoons.

9

"Can you help me with Marty's diaper?" I asked her.

"Yeah, man, I will grab the diaper bag."

We worked together quickly getting Marty changed and into his high chair for breakfast. I loved to help Mom and Dad whenever I could. It was important to me.

As we ate breakfast together, there was a knock on the door. Mom took her time walking to the door with a cigarette in her mouth. It's Dad. He walked into the apartment with a small stride. There was some other guy with him. Dad walked into the kitchen and gave hugs and kisses to the three of us. He looked so sad.

"Dad, where have you been?"

"I been working out of town, Joey. How are you?" Before I could answer, Mom interrupts.

"Terry, I need to talk to you." She said with a scowl on her face. They walked into the living room and got into a heated argument. I walked into the living room to see what was going on. I walked past this guy who came into the apartment with Dad. He was just standing against the wall not saying a word. I watched as Dad ran upstairs only to return a few moments later with his green army bag filled with what looked like clothes. He started to walk out the door when I asked, "Where are you going, Dad?"

"I am going to work, Joey. I will see you later." I looked at Toots who was sitting at the kitchen table. She was occupied with feeding Marty his breakfast.

"Toots," I said.

"What is happening?"

"I don't know, man. Come finish your breakfast." I followed Dad and his friend through the front door.

"Dad, please don't leave!"

"I have to. I love you, Joey." I looked on as he got into the passenger side of a little blue car. I turned around and walked back into the house. As I closed the door, the car drove out of sight.

I attempted to eat my cereal, but my stomach was in knots. Mom reentered the kitchen and walked over to the stove. She bent over to light yet another cigarette. She took a drag and sat down. She finished her breakfast as if all is well. Things were far from well; in fact, things will never be the same.

Every day I asked Mom when Dad was coming home. She usually would say she didn't know. What I didn't understand was why this guy Tyrone was at our apartment every day. I began to wonder if Dad was ever coming home

2
BEAR IN THE COOKIE JAR

oday was like any other Saturday. We made ourselves breakfast and watched cartoons. Surprisingly, Mom was still sleeping. That was odd. She was usually up before us, enjoying her instant coffee. Concerned about her, I said, "Toots, I am going to check on Mom."

"Okay, man, go ahead," she said. I walked upstairs and let myself into her room. I could not believe what I saw. There in all his naked glory was Tyrone next to Mom in Dad's bed. She must have heard the door open.

"What do you need, you little creep? Get out of here!" she screamed at the top of her lungs.

I ran downstairs in shock. Toots knew something was up; how could she not after hearing Mom? "Joey, what's wrong, man?"

"Tyrone is in bed with Mom." I ran outside for some fresh air. I walked around the corner and sat down on the stoop still in a state of shock. *What does this mean? Is Dad not coming back? Is this guy moving in?* I didn't have to ponder my thoughts for long. Mom opened the front door and hollered for me to come inside. She didn't sound like she was in a good mood. I entered the house to find Toots in the living room, holding Marty.

Mom was pacing back and forth, smoking a cigarette in front of Toots. As I entered the living room, Mom looked in my direction.

"Joey, get in here and have a seat!" she barked. I sat on the floor next to the chair Toots was sitting on.

"This is the deal, you two. Your Dad is not coming back. He left us. Tyrone is moving in, so deal with it. Joey, don't ask me about your dad because he is history. Do you understand?" she asked as she towers over me. I just stared at the ground. I was trying not to cry.

"Yes, I do," I responded finally as my head began to spin."

"Well that's great, Ma, just great!" Toots said as she stormed upstairs with Marty. I could no longer hold back the tears. I was left in the living room by myself, crying until I could not cry anymore. It's official. My life as I knew it was over.

Baby Greg

Greg was born on August 18. Toots and I were so excited to have another brother to spoil. Tyrone did not seem as excited as I thought he would be. I didn't know why, but things seemed a little fishy. Tyrone was living here full time. He did not work, but he sure found quality things to do with his time. He smoked Kool brand cigarettes, and drank E.J. brandy like it was water. Instead of trying to bond with the four children, he was usually playing basketball with all the other losers. He wore a pair of white Chuck Taylors. I guess he thought he was something special. No one else had money for such nice things, apparently. The professional basketball players on TV wore the same shoes. I guess he believed he was on par with those guys. Well, I wish he would take his circus act somewhere else. I was only four, but I knew a dud when I saw a dud.

Jacks

Mom and Tyrone were drinking booze and smoking weed every night. The household was in turmoil. They got into heated arguments about Dad on a regular basis. These have turned into physical altercations. I remember how Mom and Dad would have arguments about money and him not working enough to help the family. Dad always seemed to find work and stay out of Mom's hair, but I guess that was not good enough for her.

Although they would get into arguments and sometimes it turned into an actual fight, Mom would punch, kick, and bite Dad, but he would never hit back. One day, right after we moved into the new apartment, things spiraled out of control. She cornered Dad by the fridge. Mom began to flail on him. He closed his eyes and covered up. I ran toward the two of them as I hollered.

"Mom, stop!"

"Hey, you little son of a bitch. Get out of here! I will deal with you in a minute." She returned to flailing on Dad. I cried, "Please stop it!" As I watched from the living room, Mom stormed out of the kitchen, following Dad into the living room. She continued to beat Dad. Before I knew it, she stopped, grabbed her beer, and took a huge drink. She returned the beer to the table. She looked at me and said, "I am going to teach you to mind your business, brat!" I was frozen in fear as she walked in my direction.

"God, please help!"

"God can't help you, you little brat!" She hardly got the brat word out of her mouth when she grabbed me by the arm. With a cigarette in her mouth, the wooden paddle in her right hand, and fury in her eyes, she pummeled me repeatedly. She hit me as hard as she could on my back, side, and the back of the head with that piece of misery. I didn't know why she was doing this. Was it because she was drunk and angry with me, or was she just bored?

"Joey, I will tell you one time. You will never interrupt me again you, little moron." It was over just as quickly as it started. She turned from me and returned to her lair. I could hear her open the fridge, grab a beer, and open it up. I wondered if Dad was okay. I managed to walk around the corner over to the stairs. There on the floor sat Dad, bloodied and shaken up. My hero appeared to be a mere shadow of the man he once was. I ran as fast as I could up to my room, balling my eyes out. It was not because I was in pain from my own beating; I was crying for my dad. When I finally built up the courage to return downstairs, Dad was nowhere to be found. All of us kids shared the same bedroom. Whenever they got into one of these exchanges, Toots and I would take the boys to the bedroom. At least here we felt a little safe.

Toots and I loved to play "jacks." This is how it was played: Throw the ball into the air, pick up one jack, and then catch the ball after it bounces one time. Continue picking up the jacks one at a time. When you have collected all the jacks, throw them again and picking the jacks up two at a time (twosies). When you get to threesies, you must pick up the three sets of three first, then pick up the leftover jack. Continue until you are at tensies. You can then declare the winner as the first one to tens, or go back down again to onesies. Your turn continues until you miss the ball, fail to pick up the jacks, move a jack, or drop a jack that you have picked up. Your turn is then over and the next person goes. In the past, I would watch as Toots and Lisa played the game. They were both good. I have tried and have even practiced by myself. It took good hand and eye coordination, and I sucked at it. All the boys I hung around with din't play jacks. To them it was a girl's game. Toots and I were so close. If spending time with my sister meant playing jacks, I was all in. Besides, it took our minds off the chaos that went on downstairs, and my little brothers loved to watch us play.

One of the major issues with this family was the lack of love and affection that once described the family. It was nothing for Mom and Dad to shower us kids with love daily. We were very poor, but you can't buy love, and you can't fake love. Either you love or you don't. I didn't see the same affection. Mom seemed more interested in partying and making Tyrone happy. His happiness came at my expense.

Marty and Greg were growing so fast now. I wished Dad would come home. He needed to be a part of our lives. Toots was now in kindergarten, which meant I was home all day with Tyrone. Mom made it very clear to both Toots and me that since she found a job, we needed to do more around here to help Tyrone out.

3
GRAY DAYS

As time marched on, my desire to once again be reunited with Dad only grew. Marty and Greg only knew Tyrone as their father. Toots never talked about Dad, but I sensed she missed him just as much as I did. Mom was expecting another child. Her bad habits of smoking and drinking had intensified, not to mention she was mad all the time.

In short order, Mom had Leon. At first his skin was white like mine and my other siblings, but I was completely shocked as I watched his skin go from white to creamy, caramel-colored skin. I didn't understand why he looked different than the rest of us. Toots and I loved to take turns holding him. He was so cute. He had beautiful brown eyes. One night after dinner, we were sent upstairs to prepare for bed, I asked Toots as she climbed into bed, "Why does Leon look so different than Marty and Greg, man?"

"It's because Tyrone is the dad, and he is black, Joey, duh!"

"Oh," I say.

"When Dad returns, do you think he will accept him?"

"He isn't coming back. You need to give up on that idea. Tyrone befriended Dad to get to Mom. Do you really think Tyrone will let Dad around us?"

"Well, I am hoping for a miracle, Toots!"

"Dream on, dude! We are on our own. Now get to bed. We have school tomorrow.

I was seven and in second grade. Toots was eight and in third grade at Kishwaukee School. It was only a three-block walk to school every day, and it became the highlight of my day. We had the same routine each day. We met Lisa and Barry and walked together. Barry was in sixth grade. Because he was one of the biggest kids at school, I always felt safe when I was around him. Even away from school when we hung out, he watched out for me. When I arrived home after school, I helped with my brothers in any way I could. I didn't understand why Tyrone never spent time with us. For not working, he sure seemed too busy all the time. Leon was his son, but he seemed like he could care less.

I had for years stood back and watched my sister. The ability she had in caring for our brothers was remarkable. She was more of a mother than our biological mother. She was only twelve months older than me, but she had the maturity and skill set of someone much older. I learned everything from her—everything. Mom and Tyrone would go to the local bar a few nights a week, leaving Tyrone's sister Birdy to babysit. All she did was smoke cigarettes and watch TV. Toots ran the show. She was in charge.

A House Doesn't Make a Home

With the family bigger and only a two-bedroom apartment, the house had become much more cramped. It still was not, "a home." All of that changed when Dad left. It will never be a home again. In only a matter of several months after having Leon, we were approved to move into a bigger apartment. It was only a few yards from the place we were living. With it being summer, Mom and Tyrone were able to muster up help from their friends. I helped with what I could, but mostly my job was to watch the boys. They didn't take long at all to get everything moved into the new place. After the moving was finished, we went to Gerry's Hamburgers for dinner. Gerry's was my favorite place, not because of the food but because this was where Dad took me. So, I guess, the place held a special place in my heart.

After a quick dinner, we went back to the apartment. There was a lot that needed to get done over the next few days. What I was really hoping for was a fresh start with Tyrone.

4
SITTING DUCK

N ow settled into the apartment, Mom allowed me to go to the Center. I spent a few hours playing bumper pool and table tennis with Barry. Mom told me to be home by 9:00 p.m. I didn't want to leave because chances are they were drinking at home. Mom and Tyrone were far more concerned about partying whenever possible. Sure, enough as I entered through the front door, I was shocked by what I saw. I watched in horror as Tyrone was beating the crap out of Mom. He pushed her against the bathroom door and proceeded to kick her in the face. She dropped like a sack of potatoes. He would have continued to beat her if his brother Ronnie didn't pull him off her. Ronnie was as skinny as a rail. He could only weigh 160 pounds soaking wet. For the life of me, I didn't know where he got the strength to do that. He was a nice guy. He was completely different than Tyrone. He showed Mom respect and usually brought us treats on a weekly basis. He seemed genuinely interested in us kids.

"Tyrone! What are you doing to June?" Ronnie screamed at him.

"Boy, let me go. She is acting like an idiot. She bit me!" he screamed back at Ronnie. I was standing inside the front door, hoping Tyrone did not see me. For all I knew I was next on his hit list. Ronnie coaxed him over to the kitchen table where he sat down. I saw my chance to get away. I ran upstairs into Toot's bedroom where I saw her and the rest of crew all huddled on her bed. Amazingly, all the boys were sleeping.

With tears running down her cheeks, she managed to say, "Joey, I am glad you are home. They have been like this all evening."

"Are you okay, man?" I asked.

"I am okay. Help me get the kids to bed." We worked together, like many times before, to get the boys in bed. Greg, Marty, and Leon were too young to understand what was going on, which was a good thing.

One Lie Leads to Another

After we put the kids down, I followed Toots down to the kitchen to check on Ma. She was passed out on the kitchen floor, either drunk or from the beating she endured. Tyrone was pacing back and forth as Ronnie frantically attempted to wake Mom up. The look on Tyrone's face said it all. He looked scared. I secretly was hoping he would get arrested. Perhaps, he can receive a good old-fashioned beating. No such luck. Ronnie revived Ma.

She opened her eyes, raised her head, and said, "Hey, Tyrone, I am pressing charges, you freaking ape!"

"June, whatever you say, we need to get you to the ER," Ronnie said.

As she struggled to her feet and turned, I saw that her entire right side of her face was swollen. She looked like an alien, something nonhuman. I bite my bottom lip to hold back the tears. Toots put ice in a bag, and I held it on her face as she lay on her back.

"It's going to be okay, Mom. Just relax," I said as I held her hand to comfort her.

"My brothers are on their way down here, you apes! They are going to kick your asses!" Tyrone didn't respond; instead he summoned Toots and me to the kitchen table.

He looked at both of us and asked, "What happened to your mom, Joey?" *What happened to my mom?* I thought. I was afraid to say anything; I stood there frozen in fear. He began to coach us.

"I will tell you what happened: your mother was carrying a laundry basket downstairs, tripped, and fell down a whole flight of stairs." He had this habit of grinding his teeth. When he did this, you could see his jaw muscles tense up. He kept doing this the whole time he was talking to us. Maybe he thought this was a good look for him. After he went over the lie with Toots and me, he explained to Mom the importance of having the same story.

"June, you need to be consistent when you tell the doctors the story. Do you understand? I am not going to jail. If you screw this up, you will pay the price! Joey that goes for you, too! If you mess up the story, I will beat the piss right out of you! Do you understand?" I struggled to make eye contact with him on a good day. I was too terrified to look up. I knew he had me in complete fear. I managed to nod my head, and that apparently was good enough for him.

"Okay, go to bed. Ronnie is babysitting until we return. I walked into the living room to watch TV with Ronnie. He was watching some game on TV. Within five minutes, I was sound asleep.

"Joey wake up! You need to go to your bed!" he demanded. I began to stumble up the stairs. As I got closer to the top of the stairs, I could hear Mom in her room crying. I walked into her room and asked, "Mom, are you okay?"

"That ape broke my jaw, Joey, and it's all your fault!"

"Why is it my fault?" I asked bewildered and very hurt.

"He hates you. He tells me every day how you remind him of your dad. I stood up for you. It's your fault! Now get the hell out of my room!"

I was in shock. When I got to bed, I couldn't sleep. So many thoughts were racing through my mind. *My fault? My fault!* Had it come to this? It had become very clear that she had chosen him over us. To be more precise, she discarded me and left me to fend for myself. God, where are you? I need you now!

Christmas Blues

On December 3, we welcomed Andre into the world. When Mom and Tyrone returned home with the newest family member, we flocked to the front door to get a glimpse of him. He was so small.

He looked like a doll, so perfect. He had straight black hair that was so soft.

"His hair feels like silk," Toots remarked after touching him for the first time. I couldn't get over how much different he looked compared to Leon. Marty and Greg resemble each other, with blonde hair and blue-grey eyes. They were around the same size as well. The biggest difference was that Marty wore black-framed glasses. Because of his looks, combined with the fact that he liked to draw and color and keep to himself, he was dubbed "Professor," a name that fit him well. Greg was more outgoing like Toots. He liked to spend time with Steve. He was a black boy who lived next door. Steve had an older brother Tom and a sister Amy. Tom and Amy were much older than me. Ever since we moved next to that family, they have been very kind to us. Tom had invited me over on several occasions to just hang out. He was so tall for just being a teenager. He was perhaps six feet, two inches tall and thin as a rail.

A week after Andre was born, Mom sent me over to Trudy's. Trudy was Alan's mother.

"Joey, go ask Trudy if I can borrow a cup of sugar"

"Alright, Ma." I was always embarrassed to beg the neighbors for anything. Often, I was the one Mom or Tyrone sent to ask for various items. I didn't bother to put my coat on. What's the point? She lived right next door.

I knocked on Trudy's door. The door flew open.

"Hi, baby! Where is your coat?"

"I didn't think I needed it."

"Well, come in, honey," she said with a huge smile. She was a dark-skinned black woman, small in stature but with a heart as big as God's green earth.

I followed her into the apartment and up the three stairs just inside the front door. She led me into the kitchen.

"Tom is not here, baby. That's why you are here, right?" she asked as she sat at the kitchen table.

"No ma'am. Mom wants to borrow a cup of sugar."

"Oh okay. Go sit down in the living room. I will get that for you."

"Okay."

As I walked into the living room, I saw it. In the middle of the room was a huge Christmas tree. It was decorated with ornaments and tinsel and sitting on top was a beautiful star. It was covered with a ton of Christmas lights, blinking off and on. It was so gorgeous! I have seen trees this beautiful on TV but never in real life. In fact, we have never had a tree. Mom and Tyrone promised to get one, but it never happened.

I was hypnotized by the lights on the tree when Trudy called me back into the kitchen.

"'Here is the sugar, baby. Tell your mama I said hello."

Later, that evening, Mom and all of us kids were sitting in the living room watching *Charlie Brown Christmas* when Tyrone barged through the front door. Toots, Marty, and Greg ran over to greet him. I looked on from the couch, holding Leon on my lap.

"Mama gave us a bunch of Christmas tree lights and ornaments for the Christmas tree," he bellowed as he carried a huge cardboard box into the kitchen. Mom jumped up and walked toward him to inspect the box of goodies. Toots, Marty, and Greg were so excited. I was excited, too, but I contained myself. To me, it was not Christmas without Dad.

I heard Mom ask, "What are you doing with all of this crap? We don't have a tree."

"Tomorrow we are going to get a tree, June."

"With what money, huh?"

"Mama gave me money for a tree." All I can think is *he will blow the money on weed or booze*. There is no need to believe otherwise.

When I got home from school on Friday, I saw Toots getting in the car with Tyrone. I ran up to the passenger's side of the car.

As Toots rolled down her window, I asked, "Where are you going, Toots?"

"We are going to get a Christmas tree, Joey."

"Get in the house and help your mom with the kids," Tyrone demanded. I stepped back from the car as Toots rolled up her window.

She mouthed the words "Sorry, man."

I helped Mom with whatever she needed. I focused on playing with my brothers and not on the fact that Tyrone had snubbed me again. My brothers gave me so much joy. No matter what else was going on, they had a way of turning my sadness to joy.

Eventually, Tyrone returned with a huge tree. Ronnie was helping him to bring it into the house. Mom had cleared a corner in the living room to set it up. Once they got it standing up and in the tree stand, the decorating began. The three adults began to decorate the tree. My sister and brothers were glad to help with whatever. I was content watching after Leon and Andre. Leon was too small to help, and Andre was only weeks old. It felt like my folks didn't want me around. I would just be in their way

When the adults were content with how the tree looked, they all retreated to the kitchen. Within seconds, I could hear cans opening—not just any cans but beer cans. *Are you serious?* I thought. I walked into the kitchen; sure enough, they were sitting around the little table, guzzling beers. I walked back into the living room. My arms were heavy from holding Andre. He was sound asleep. I went upstairs to put him in his crib. Just as I covered him up, Tyrone shouted up the stairs.

"Joey, get down here, boy!"

"I am coming," I said. I ran down the stairs as fast as I could. Tyron was standing in front of the tree, admiring his handiwork. The tree did look nice. For our first tree, it would do. When I walked up in front of Tyrone, he stared at me with a devilish grin.

"It is your job to put water in the tree stand every day. Also, you need to pick up the pine needles off the floor. If you don't follow these simple tasks, you will get a whooping! Is that understood, boy?"

"Yes, sir," I said. I looked over to Ma expecting her to defend me. I mean, why was this solely my job, anyway?

She looked at me in her drunken state and said, "Make yourself useful, moron!"

I stood there with my head down, staring at the ground. When they returned to the kitchen, I made my way to bed.

Christmas Morning

When Toots and I got up, we woke up the boys and flew downstairs as fast as we could to open our gifts. Toots and I pulled all the gifts from under the tree to pass them out to the boys. As soon as I got the boys all their gifts, I focused my attention on the gifts awaiting me.

"Toots, where did you put my gifts? I didn't see any with my name on it."

"Over there, Joey; that's yours." Just as Toots said, there were my gifts—all three of them in pretty paper. It made them seem so big. Three gifts here must be a mistake. Everyone else had much more. Maybe Ma put Marty's name on my gifts, an honest mistake.

"Toots, are you sure this is all I got?"

"Yeah, Joey, now open your gifts." I decided before I opened my gifts, I needed to investigate this thing more. Maybe someone was enjoying toys that are intended for me. I tried to be real slick with my intentions, not to cause any problems. Before I could put my plan into motion, trouble showed up.

Unaware of Mom's presence, I began to snoop around Marty's things to see if indeed he had my toys by mistake.

"Joey, what in the hell are you doing? Leave Marty's toys alone!"

"I am just seeing if maybe someone got our gifts messed up."

"Joey, how many gifts did you get?"

"Three, Ma."

"That's right then; that's all you got was three gifts, no mix up! The little ones got more toys since you are the oldest boy, you need to just deal with it!" *Okay, so why does Toots have toys coming out of her ears?* I thought. Yep, it is official. Ma had been sold out to Tyrone's grand plan. This was just plain unfair. I had felt short-changed before, but this cut me to the core.

I remembered sharing a Christmas with Mom and Dad. That holiday had been a fun time back during the pre-Tyrone days. Now, everything has changed. Dad was gone. Mom had changed. Life was getting worse. Toot's birthday was just before Christmas, and mine was just ten days after New Year's. Mom invited every one of Toot's friends to her birthday party. There was ice cream, cake, and a cool party. The works! I was so happy for her. I couldn't wait for my celebration in only a few short weeks.

My birthday came and went with no Happy Birthday. No cake, no party or celebration—nothing. Great, doesn't anyone care? Did Ma get so busy she just forgot?

Easter Day

Easter Sunday was the only day I can recall the whole family going to church together. We went to Emmanuel Temple for the service. It was a small African American church. The people seemed very nice. I recognized many faces from Jane Addams throughout the sanctuary. We heard the preacher give a hell-and-brimstone message, which was kind of spooky. I thought it made Tyrone a bit uncomfortable because he did not want to stick around for the free meal afterward. I certainly did, and both Ma and Tyrone said I could. Thank God, another chance to stay away a little bit longer. Everyone else went home, leaving me to fend for myself. No problem; I have grown accustomed to that. I relished it, and I am not far from home. So, there was no problem from my perspective.

I ate to my heart's content. The folks that made this food sure knew how to cook. I sure wish they would do this more often because I would be here to enjoy it. When it got to be time to head home, I thanked all the nice folks for everything and walked home. I made a beeline to the apartment. As soon as I got home, it appeared that Tyrone was upset about something again. I could always tell when he was in a foul mood. He paced around the apartment, talking to himself. I decided to make myself scarce by going to the basement. To my surprise, Toots and the boys were already down there watching TV.

"Hey Toots, what are you doing, man?"

"Just watching a little TV. Did you have fun at the church dinner?"

"I had a great time. Man, was the food good!"

"Dad was here."

"Dad was here? When? How did he look; how long was he here?"

"Tyrone would not let him in the house, and I only saw him for a second standing at the door. He left something for you."

"Where is it?"

"Tyrone has it." Great, not only am I separated from Dad, but when he really wants to see his kids, Tyrone would not let him. It was so unfair.

I hung out with Toots and the crew until I thought it would be safe to venture upstairs. I wanted to claim my gift from Dad. I wondered what it is.

"Toots, did he give you anything?"

"Yeah man, but Tyrone has that, too. Who knows when we will get it?" More than anything I was wishing I could have seen Dad. It has been so long since I was last with him. I really missed him.

The next morning, I woke up earlier than usual, hoping to talk to Ma about the visit from Dad. Why he was denied access to his kids? Thankfully, Tyrone was nowhere around, so I felt I could freely talk to her. She was sitting at the kitchen table, drinking her coffee.

"Ma, why didn't you tell me Dad was in town?"

"He is a drifter, a hobo, Joey. He travels all over the country, and I had no idea he was in town for your information!"

"I hate that I missed him, but if he comes back, do you think I can spend some time with him?"

"Why? Your dad left me with all of you kids to fend for myself! Why should I let him see you? He doesn't send money, and when he showed up yesterday, he was drunk. Joey, don't get your hopes up on seeing your dad anytime soon. Maybe you will see him again in the summer when you go to Dubuque. Oh, before I forget, he left this for you. He said it was your birthday gift."

"Thanks, Ma." That's was all I could muster. Thanks for nothing. You are so far up Tyrone's butt it was not funny. I was sure she probably had lied about dad being drunk yesterday just to make him look bad. I found it hard to believe he would drink before coming to see us.

Ma handed me a crumpled-up brown bag that had seen better days with something bulky inside of it. Ma just sat there expecting me to rip the bag open, but instead I ran upstairs into my room. I ever so carefully opened it up. There it was, the "Jaws" necklace. Ever since the movie came out, I had seen other kids wearing the necklace. It was in the shape of a shark head with all the teeth protruding out of its mouth—so cool. I had asked Ma if she would buy me one, but the answer was always, "Hell, no!" How did Dad know I wanted that necklace? No matter, I had one now and it came from *my dad*. I was so happy; I wore it every day around the 'hood to the envy of my friends.

5
HARD CHARGING

S ummer, was finally here and my excitement to go to Dubuque only grew, Mom busted that bubble! She reneged on allowing me to go to Dubuque. I stayed out of her and Tyrone's way as much as possible. I stayed busy with chores around the house, which was the common theme with me and Tyrone—"Seen but not heard." The process was, I am seen doing my chores without complaining. In fact, I did them without speaking to him unless he spoke to me first. Summer flew by in a flash. Before I knew it, school was right around the corner.

I started third grade at Kishwaukee. The first few days were a breeze. I was so glad to be back in school because it was more than books and rules. It was an "out" for me—a way to get out of the house. I wanted to do my best in school, so I can make something of my life. All around the neighborhood there was poverty, crime, prostitution, and drug use. I knew one thing. I didn't want to end up like those folks with no future. I also knew I would not find direction at home from my parents. It only made it that much clearer. I needed to excel in school, so I didn't end up like Ma or Tyrone.

Toots and I were both enrolled in some after-school activities at a neighborhood church twice a week. Toots went to charm school, and I went to Good Grooming (G.G.) on Monday afternoons. On Tuesdays, we both went to Bible club at the same church. I really enjoyed going to the clubs; besides, I could stay away from Tyrone that much more. I could truly bond with Toots; it was a dream come true. Some of our closest friends were there, too: Lisa, Mark, and Antonio. We had a lot of fun. Mary, our instructor, was so kind. She was a heavy-set woman with brown hair and glasses.

What's the catch? She's being nice for what? Nobody is this nice for free was the thought racing through my mind. *She is up to some trick; I've seen this before.* As time went on, I discovered Mary was always sincere and very nice toward me. Could there really be other people out there who cared about us? I could not wait for Monday and Tuesday to get here. Most kids I knew could not wait for the weekend but not me. I was onto something here, something good, something that was helping me see the way things should be.

One night, when we got home late due to club, we arrived only to find Ma and Tyrone not home. Birdy was babysitting the boys.

"Joey, where you been boy?"

"I was at Bible club, why?"

"Your Mama asked me to babysit these bad-ass boys, so I need your help. Don't go running off to the Center!"

Whatever, I thought. Here was a grown woman who said she needed my help, yeah right! She was just lazy. I guess she thought I would be her boy to do all the work, and she got paid for nothing.

"Where's my ma?"

"Your Mama and Daddy went down to the Elk's." Oh wonderful, here we were with Tyrone's crazy sister and no food in the house. They had to go get drunk at the bar with the money that should have been used for food. This was not right. I needed to do something to help my family out.

The Sandwich Factory was a local restaurant near the projects. I would walk through their parking lot when I would go to Park It Market. Often, I would see my friends with their families going there to eat. We never had the pleasure of eating there. Mom would always say,

"We don't have money for eating out. Make a bologna sandwich!" I could not help but notice how much garbage would be scattered throughout the restaurant property, like beer cans, cigarette butts, and candy wrappers. You name it, and it was there, not to mention the front of the store's glass door was filthy.

One day, after I walked home from school, I decided to stop by to ask if I could get a job. I mean maybe if I could earn money, I could help Mom buy food. I was determined to at least try.

I walked through the front door. Behind the counter was a teenage girl.

"Hey kid, can I help you?"

"Yes, I am wondering if I can get a job here?"

"Hi, I am Babe. I am sorry, honey, but you are way too young."

"Okay, take care." I said as I turned around and walked out. Just as I got to the sidewalk, I heard a voice behind me.

"Hey, kid, wait!" I turned to see who hollered at me. There was Babe with an older man.

"Hey, kid, do you need a job? I need someone to pick up my parking lot and sweep it. If you do a good job, I will pay you well." I made my way back to where Babe and the older man were standing.

"I will do it. Can I work every day? We need the money."

"Let's start by telling me your name."

"My name is Joey."

"Nice to meet you, Joey. I am Bob. I own this joint. How old are you?"

"I am eight, sir."

"Very good. I will show you what I need you to do every Saturday. I will pay you two dollars each time." I was so excited to have a job.

Bob walked me through the duties in no time flat. After he showed me where I could get the supplies, he gave me a can of soda. As I sat across from him at one of the tables he said.

"One more thing son. This job will not help much with your family's situation. You are just a child; it is not your place to be concerned with this matter. What this job will do for you is give you a little spending money to buy something you want. I am impressed with your attitude and commitment to this job. If you do good work, I will give you a raise," he stated emphatically. After I drank my soda, I made my way to the door.

"Thanks, Bob, and thank you, Babe. I will see you later."

"Tomorrow, kid. You work tomorrow. It is Saturday," Babe said.

31

"Oh, yeah. I will be here; bye." Not only did I have my first job, I was in love with Babe. She was gorgeous. She had green eyes, brown hair, and was tall. I made it home, daydreaming about my future as a Sandwich Factory employee and maybe even Babe's boyfriend.

I woke up the next morning. Instead of joining the other kids for our ritual of cartoon bonanza, I made my way to my job. I told Ma all the details. She was okay with me doing this. After all, it may lead to a longtime full-time job. I was surprised, to be honest, that she was so easygoing about it. Now there was nothing to it than to do it.

6
BAD PENNY

June was here, and there were only a few days left of school. In the past, we would begin to pack our things for our summer stay in Dubuque. We would wash and gas up the car, check, and recheck to make sure we had all that we would need for our trip. This time was different, though. After the last day of school with my report card in hand, I ran home as fast as I could, so we could begin vacation. Ma met me in the front yard with a funny look on her face.

"Joey, there has been a change of plans." With that exchange, she walked into the house without telling me the change. Oh great, they are not going to let me go. I passed all my classes; I have been doing what I was told by both Ma and Tyrone. What gives? I found Ma at the stove lighting a cigarette.

"Ma, here is my report card. What is going on?"

"We are taking you and Toots to the Greyhound. You guys are catching the bus to Dubuque." I have never taken a bus ride to Dubuque before, but to me it sounds like a good thing. At least I won't have to worry about the bus driver drinking and driving! I followed Ma into the living room where she looked over my report card. She didn't say a word, just silence.

"Good job, son" was in order, I thought for a moment before I snapped back to reality. She usually gave me the cold shoulder routine. To acknowledge my accomplishments would be too normal

around here. I knew this: had I failed one class, she would not let me get on that bus.

There was a bus heading for Dubuque at five, which didn't give me much time to get there. Not to worry though; I was sure Tyrone wanted me on that bus just as much as I did. I was confident he would get us there on time for a change. He didn't disappoint, and before long we were waving goodbye through the window on the bus. Dubuque, here we come. I slept most of the way just to wake as we were crossing the bridge over the Mississippi River. Almost like clockwork I could smell the bread from the bakery below. I took a deep breath, thanking God for one more time in Dubuque.

A Change of Pace

Our grandparents picked us up at seven on the button. Boy, were they a sight for sore eyes.

"Toots, Joey, how are you kids?" Toots responded matter of fact, "I am much better now!'"

"Me, too. I sure missed you guys!" I put my bag in the trunk and crawled to the back seat ready to have some fun. I really missed my dad.

"Grandpa, is Dad in town?" I asked eagerly.

"Nope, I don't know where your dad is, Joey, but we will make some calls." I was happy to see my grandparents, but the person I really yearned for is nowhere around. As we got to the house, Toots and I unloaded our bags. Walter greeted us as we headed into the house.

"Hey, Joey, Hi, Toots, you guys are sure getting big. Joey, take your bags up to the attic, you will be sleeping up there. I will help you guys in a second. I need to go to the bathroom." Cool, I got to sleep in the attic, which was more like an open loft where Uncle Frank's bedroom was. Toots slept up there, too, but I didn't think she liked all the stuffed eagles and owls staring down at her.

Once we got all settled in, Gram fed us supper and then off to bed. I slept like a rock; I was so tired. When I finally wake, Toots was nowhere around. I keow she must have been tired as well, but maybe she didn't sleep well in a different bed. I threw on my clothes and headed downstairs to catch some chow.

"We are in the living room, Joey," Grandma called out. I walked through the kitchen into the living room where I found my grandparents, Toots, and Uncle Walter sitting around visiting.

"We already ate, but there is a plate in the fridge for you."

"Thanks." After I ate my breakfast, Grandpa gathered Toots and me to reassure us that we were safe here. We didn't need to worry about being mistreated. Toots and I both knew that, but it was nice to know our grandparents understood that was a concern of ours.

Somehow, some way, Aunt Grace got in touch with Dad. Toots had gone to spend time with my aunt Dorothy. I felt bad that she would not be around when Dad showed up.

At Long Last

During breakfast the next morning, Sissy began to bark as someone walked through the front door "The bad penny has returned," Dad said as he entered the kitchen.

"Dad!" I exclaimed as I bolted from the table and into his arms. I could smell the cologne he had on. It was the same smell I remembered as a little child.

"Hi, Joey," he said with a big smile on his face.

"Hi, Dad. I love you. Hey! Toots is here; she is at Dorothy's."

"Okay, well Frank is going to lend me his jeep, so finish breakfast and we can go."

"Okay," I said. I finished my breakfast in no time flat. My grandparents seemed as excited as I was by the look on their faces. They knew how much I missed my dad. In fact, I was certain I drove them nuts inquiring about his whereabouts on a regular basis.

Frank showed up a short time later. He motioned for Dad to come into the living room where he was standing. There he gave Dad some instructions about the jeep, and then we were off. Dad drove all over Dubuque on this beautiful day. The first place we went was Eagle Point Park. It was so pretty. The park overlooked the Mississippi River. After an hour of taking in the sights, he drove downtown to my favorite spot—the elevator on Fourth Street. Dad had taken me here once before. This time was more special. I hoped this day would never end.

Near the end of our trip, Dad asked, "So what do you want to do now?"

"I don't know, Dad; I just want to spend time with you!" I replied. Dad seemed a little rusty at the wheel; I could tell he was nervous about driving. In fact, when we were turning right at a red light, Dad did not yield. A huge semi almost creamed us.

"Look out!"

"Oops," was his only response.

"Joey, do you want to go somewhere for dinner?"

"Yeah, I'm starving like Marvin."

"Okay. We will just go to Don's Tavern for dinner. They have good burgers."

"Isn't that the bar Grandpa goes to with all of the weird animals mounted on the walls?"

"Yeah, but don't worry, kid, Grandpa won't be there. This is our time. Don's is one of my favorite places in all of Dubuque."

Up until this point, Dad had not even once asked about Toots, Marty, or Greg. I was confused by that behavior. After all of the time apart from his kids, I expected him to ask me a lot of questions. Maybe I was wrong about this, but since Dad never developed a bond with the youngest children, he had the mindset of "Out of sight, out of mind."

Once we arrived at Don's on the south end of Dubuque, Dad wasted no time as he made his way up to the bar. He ordered a beer. I sat down next to him, eagerly waiting for him to order us lunch.

After Dad drank his third beer, I asked him.

"Can I get something to eat, Dad?"

"What do you want?"

"I'll take a cheeseburger and fries, please." Dad summoned the bartender and placed the order, but he forgot to order for himself.

"Dad, you forgot to order something for yourself— aren't you hungry?"

"No, I am going to play the jukebox instead." Don's had a jukebox that had seen better days. Dad was a huge Elvis Presley fan. Once he found some Elvis songs on the jukebox, all the patrons were in for a treat.

Content with his musical selections, he walked back to the bar just as my food arrived. Dad really liked beer. I began to eat my food when I sneaked a look at Dad.

"Do you want some of the food, Dad? I can't eat all of this." Dad was snapping his fingers in time with the music, oblivious to me. I tapped him on his shoulder to get his attention. He looked at me with the same look Mom had whenever she got drunk.

"Joey, I told you before I am not hungry. Let's move over to a booth so I can be closer to the jukebox." I followed Dad over to the only table near the jukebox.

Dad was spending more time at the jukebox than visiting with me. Some of those songs he selected revive memories from when we were all together as a family. Tom Jones, Johnny Cash, and others were played repeatedly back in those days. That music was a big part of who Dad was. We did not have much materially, but we were together. I realized even though our family was torn apart, he still had this music he enjoyed so much. It seemed to ease his pain.

I became concerned about Dad's behavior. He had become very loud and rude toward me.

"Dad, can we go home?"

"We will leave when the bar closes, son." He reached into his wallet and retrieved a one-dollar bill.

"Go to the bar and buy a soda. I am going to play some more music." Instead of buying a soda, I asked the bartender for change to make a phone call. I found a pay phone and called Grandpa.

"We are at Don's. Dad is drunk. Can you come pick me up?"

"I will be right there. Don't let your dad drive!"

"I won't."

I had grown accustomed to being around Mom and Tyrone when they were drunk. It was different with Dad, but I knew I must get him home before something worse happened Within ten minutes, Grandpa walked into the bar. He made a beeline to our table. Dad was too busy drinking to notice the visitor. I studied Grandpa's face as he walked toward us. He looked very mad. I have never seen Grandpa mad about anything. He usually had a smile on his face. He was not as talkative as Grandma, but I loved spending time with him. Dad staggered once again to the jukebox.

Grandpa stood between him and the jukebox and said, "Is this what you planned to do with your son who you have not seen in a very long time? Give me the car keys!" he snapped. Dad turned away from him and came back to the table. There were two full beers sitting at the table. He proceeded to slam one and then the second.

"Okay, Joey, let's go! It's time to take you back to Grandma's" I was getting really scared.

"Is Dad going to drive in this condition?"

"Terry, you are not driving anywhere! Give me the car keys!" I watched as Dad reluctantly handed over the keys.

"Joey, go outside and get in my truck"

"Okay. Bye, Dad," I yelled as I rushed outside. I looked back at Dad as I ran out through the door. He was slumped over the jukebox. Grandpa was telling him something, but I couldn't hear it over the music.

Once I found the truck, I climbed in the passenger's side. It was a gold Ford F100. Grandpa was a steeplejack by trade. He painted church bell towers, water towers, and practically anything that no one else wanted to paint. It was a very dangerous job, working hundreds of feet in the air. It sounded really scary to me, but he seemed to love it. In the back of his truck were all the tools of the trade: ladders, paint, paint rollers, and so on. I loved this truck because of whose it was. When I climbed into the passenger seat, there was a strong order of cigar smoke. It was weird, but I liked it. Grandpa finally walked out of the bar. He appeared to be crying. I had never seen this side of him before. As Grandpa got behind the wheel, I watched for Dad to show up as well. Grandpa started the truck and began to pull out of the parking lot.

"Is Dad coming?"

"No, honey, he's not. I need to get you home."

Once home, I took a bath and went to bed. I tossed and turned for hours worried about what Dad was doing. Was he still at the bar or in jail? I finally decided to go downstairs where Grandpa was watching TV with Grandma.

"Is Dad going to be okay? Is he coming here tonight?"

"No, honey, hopefully he will go to the Mission. I need to get in touch with Frank. His jeep is still at the bar," Grandpa said. "Why won't you let him stay here?" I asked.

"We are too old to be dealing with Terry's drunken antics, honey," Grandma said.

"Don't you love my dad? What if something bad happens to him out there?" I asked through the tears.

"Honey, he will be fine. I am sure he will be around once he sobers up," Grandpa said.

"I am going to bed." I laid in my bed crying my eyes out. Before long, Grandma came up to check on me.

"I am sorry, Joey. Tomorrow will be better; get some sleep."

7
CHUMMY TIMES

The next morning, I woke up to a pleasant surprise. Grace and the girls were downstairs visiting with my grandparents. Grandma made a huge breakfast. It was so nice to see everyone. I silently wondered where Dad was. After breakfast, Paula and I took Sissy to the woods. When we finally got down to Dead Man's Cave, Paula asked "So, are you excited about coming to our house to stay?"

"Yeah, I am, but I'm not looking forward to going back to Rockford!"

What are you talking about, Joey? You are coming to stay with us for good. Mom is going to adopt you." My jaw dropped to the ground when I heard what Paula shared with me.

"That's not funny, Paula!"

"If you don't believe me, Joey, just ask Mom."

I often dreamed of being a part of Grace's immediate family ever since it seemed like Dad was out of the picture for good. I never thought in a million years this idea of her adopting me would ever be possible. I ran up the remainder of the hill as fast as I could, leaving her in my wake.

I barged into the living room where I found Grace and my grandparents in one of their serious conversation about someone but who? I didn't care at this point.

"Grace, am I going to live with you and the girls? Are you going to adopt me?"

"Settle down, Joey, we need to talk. Go back outside while I talk to Grandma and Grandpa."

"Okay." I went out to the front stoop and waited for Grace to come out. I was experiencing a multitude of emotions.

Was this real? Was I dreaming? Could it be that I was free from the nightmare? Please, God, let Grace adopt me. I could hear someone open the door and walk out onto the stoop behind me.

Grace sat next to me on the stoop and proceeded to tell me, "Joey, your mom and dad have agreed to let me adopt you. They both feel it would be better for you if you were raised in Dubuque. I know you will miss your sister and brothers, but my girls love you. They can't wait for you to become their brother—that is—if you agree to the adoption."

I was in total shock. I just couldn't believe someone would go through all those steps to have me in their lives. I have always been treated as a second-class person at home, never feeling like I belonged. It seems too good to be true.

"We are waiting for your mother to sign the paperwork to make it official. Until then, I want you to come and stay with us."

"Thank you, Grace, I love you!"

"I love you, too, honey."

Time spent at Grace's went so fast. She always took time to tell me she loved me. She also demonstrated this by the way she treated me. Grace lived in a big white house on Washington Street near Comisky Park. I spent a lot of time at the park; it was a lot of fun playing with Grace's girls. When we were not in the park, we role-played in the neighborhood. I was the mailman. Grace found an old canary yellow purse she said I could have. I was not a very good mailman without a mailbag! I stuffed pieces of scrap paper inside of it. Now it was my job to deliver the mail. I rode a little red bike door-to-door, delivering the mail. It was so much fun! I felt so safe, so free, here.

Many times, Paula would get all dolled up with her sister Patty, and they would pretend to be "Miss America" and strut around the neighborhood. The sidewalk was their runway. Patty had a summer tan, black hair, and brown eyes. Paula also had a dark summer tan. She had brown hair and beautiful brown eyes as well. I was one of the judges, and Grace was the other judge. Both Patty and Paula were so pretty; it was hard to pick a winner. They always draw a crowd of other kids on the block. When the event was over, it was time to crown a winner. Grace had fashioned a crown out of aluminum foil. Paula was always the crowd favorite. I guess it was her friendly persona. I didn't want to upset them, so I said, "It's a tie." Everyone was happy that way.

Stacy was the middle daughter. She had dirty blonde hair and brown eyes. She did not get involved in the fashion show. Instead she liked to take me on long bike rides in the neighborhood. She was good on a bike. She had these streets memorized. She led me through a maze of streets and alleys. I loved hanging out with her. We were both eight years old. She was very funny and smart for her age. One morning, when I woke up, I went downstairs. I saw my dad sitting at the kitchen table with Grace. I ran into the kitchen to greet Dad.

"Hi, Dad. Where have you been?"

"I have been living all over the place. I have some good news for you! I want you to sit down. I have agreed to let Grace adopt you. I have signed all the paperwork, and we are just waiting for your mom to complete the necessary steps on her end. Your mom thought you would be much better off in this situation. I would love nothing more than to get you away from Tyrone."

"What about Toots and my brothers?"

"You'll see them in the summer and on holidays. Patty, Stacy, and Paula will be your sisters now, so you won't be alone."

Patty chimed in, "Yeah, Joey, why do you think we went through all the trouble of fixing your room for you to stay? We would love it if you lived with us."

"In the meantime, Joey, you need to listen to Grace, and help her as much as possible around here."

This was all way too much for me to take in at once. On one hand, I was hopefully away from that monster Tyrone forever, but I couldn't bear the thought of being away from my siblings.

"Okay, guys, come get some breakfast." Grace said. Just as I poured milk over my cereal, Dad said, "Hurry up and eat your breakfast, Joey; we are going to see someone special!" I ate the cereal quickly, so I could enjoy every minute I had with my dad. It had been over two weeks since I saw him last. I really missed him. Dad was standing over me now, jingling a set of keys.

"Whose keys are those, Dad?"

"Grace's. She is going to let me borrow her car. Grace had a late model Chevy Nova. It was dark blue with black seats. It was a cool car. She kept it real neat and clean, unlike our car back in Rockford. We had a sky-blue Rambler station wagon. I hated riding in the Rambler because I would always get stuck sitting right behind Tyrone. Toots and my brothers could sit wherever they wanted.

Now finished with breakfast, I followed Dad out to the car. He seemed to be in a hurry. At least the car had an automatic transmission. Dad really struggled driving Frank's manual transmission.

As Dad pulled out I asked, "Where are we going, Dad?"

"We are going to see your Aunt Dorothy." She was one of Ma's older sisters, who lived on the north end on 32nd street. It only took about five minutes before I was sitting in Dorothy's kitchen.

Too Good to Be True

As Dad and Dorothy sat in the kitchen yapping away, I searched high and low for Toots, but there was no Toots anywhere.

"Dorothy, where is Toots?"

"She went shopping with Jane and Donna."

I really missed Toots, and I know before long she would be going back home. If all went according to the plan, I would be staying with Grace from now on. Dorothy soon took my mind off Toots when she produced a plate full of goodies: Twinkies, Ho Hoes, chips, and more. What a good day this is turning into. I helped myself to the snacks and went outside to enjoy my sugar feast. After I wolfed down the snacks, I made my way back into the house where Dorothy and Dad were having a conversation.

"Why are you so happy, Terry? I haven't seen you this upbeat in years."

He laughs.

"I have some good news. Grace has agreed to adopt Joey, and all we are waiting for is for June to sign the paperwork."

"You mean to tell me that you are giving up all of your rights to Joey?"

"Hell, yeah. June is with that loser Tyrone, and we all know how Tyrone abuses Joey physically and emotionally. Since I am not in a position right now to take care of my kids, this is the next best thing."

"Joey have a seat, I'm making a call to June to find out what is going on with your mom."

"What do you mean, Dorothy?"

"I can't believe your mom is just going to give you up to your Aunt Grace!" I sat down as a terrible thought began racing through my mind. *Why is Dorothy ruining all of our best-laid plans?*

It wasn't long before Dorothy was on the phone, dialing up Ma. Dad had a real sick look on his face that didn't sit well with me at all; maybe he knows something I didn't.

"Joey, go into my bedroom and pick up the other phone, so you can talk to your mom," Dorothy demanded. I walk into the bedroom, not knowing what I will hear on the other end of the phone.

"Hi Ma, how are you doing?"

"Good, how are you?"

"Good, having fun with Dad and Grace."

"Hey, Joey, is Toots there? I need to talk to her."

"No, June, she isn't here, you simpleton!" Dorothy screamed from the other phone in the kitchen.

"Oh, hey, Dorothy, I didn't know you liked to listen in on other people's conversations.

"Shut your yap. What is this crap about you giving up your kid?"

"Joey is going to live with Grace. Things just have not worked out. I have tried everything with him."

"Sure, June, why don't you just admit it—Tyrone hates him, and he has convinced you to ship him off. That is your child, you little tramp! I don't care how bad things may be right now—you don't throw your kids away. You better not go through with this adoption thing, or I will make a trip down there to knock some sense into your head, simpleton!"

I am standing here in utter disbelief. I just wanted Ma to say anything, anything at all, to shut Dorothy up. I am so ready to stay in Dubuque with Grace, but now, things are a little dicey.

"June, what's wrong? Cat got your tongue?" *Click*. Ma hangs up. Thanks for nothing, Ma, as usual. This is her way of saying "screw you." Don't worry about what I am doing or was it that Dorothy struck a nerve, and she is reconsidering her opinions? Time would tell.

After our short phone conversation with Ma, Uncle Jake asks Dad and me to stay for dinner. I could tell by the way Dorothy was acting that she didn't want us to stay. The tension in the room is high. I thought the phone call really caused everything to intensify. Dad and I pass on dinner and head back over to Grace's place. I can tell he is devastated by the turn of events that transpired at Dorothy's; it is written all over his face. Up until this point, I thought becoming Grace's adopted son is as good as done, but I have a sick feeling in my stomach that things are about to change.

8
UPSIDE DOWN

On Sunday afternoon, Grandma had all of us up for dinner. She was such a good cook, and all her kids enjoy spending time there, so much so that it is a routine for the whole family to spend Sundays at Grandma's house.

Grace is always running late, but on this occasion, she is the first to arrive. We are greeted at the door by Grandpa. He said, "Hi, you" —his signature hello. Grandma made spaghetti and noodles, one of my favorite meals. Boy, is it good. After dinner, we all sat around in the little living room making small talk about all the fun things we did this summer. The phone interrupts our time. It is Ma, and she wants to talk to me. *Oh boy*, I thought. *Is she going to be in a good mood or mad at the world?*

"Hi, Ma."

"Hi, Joey, Tyrone and I are coming to Dubuque tomorrow to pick up you and Toots. You need to be at your grandmas, so I don't have to drive all over town trying to track you down."

"What! I thought I was staying!"

"No, Joey, you are coming back with us. Let me talk to your aunt Grace. She is there, isn't she?" I am devastated. I hand the phone to Grace and go to the basement to be alone. I am crying my eyes out, trying to understand what has just transpired. I can hear Grace on the phone with Ma; it doesn't sound like Grace is very happy with the whole situation, either. Paula comes downstairs to check on me. She is standing at the bottom of the stairs.

"Joey, I am sorry."

"I really want to be left alone, Paula," I snap at her.

"Okay, Joey, I just want to say I love you, and if you need to hang out, I will be around."

"Thanks, Paula." After some time, I can't hold it anymore; I must use the bathroom.

As I walk upstairs, Grandma stops me in the kitchen, "We love you, Joey. I am sorry that you can't stay, but just know we are here for you."

Boy, I thought I was done being upset about this whole thing, but after that exchange with her, the floodgates really opened.

"I don't want to go back there. Tyrone hates me. He beats me all the time, and Ma lets it happen. Please, Grandma, can I stay with you? Can you talk some sense to my ma?"

"I tried, Joey. Grace and I both talked to her, but she is backing out of the adoption. I'm afraid she has her mind set on bringing you back with her. I'm so sorry." I have that awful feeling in my stomach again. I am going back to the trenches with my only way out of that hellhole now gone.

Early the next morning Grace asks me to come downstairs to breakfast. I don't want to move. I know that I have no choice. I begin to pack my things when the girls come into my room. Patty, Paula, and Stacy help me pack my bags.

After we ate breakfast, we played in the backyard for a time. I really wasn't in a playful mood. I was melancholy. I found myself really taking everything in—the way Grace's house looked and smelled like cookies, how the back yard looked, the little quirks of my cousins, and just the love I experienced from everyone. Love is a good thing, and the love in this home is the genuine article.

Leaving Town

As Grace drives up to Grandmas, I am as quiet as a mouse, taking in all the sites because I know that I would never be back. I will miss Dubuque, but most of all, I will miss my relatives here. I just wonder what it would have been like to be Grace's son. I am hoping and praying that Dad will be there to bring an end to this whole idea of me going back to Rockford with the beast. I have not seen him for the last few days. He has a bad habit of just taking off without saying a word, but this time is different. If Dad is at Grandmas, I know that he would try to convince Mom to let me stay. I kept asking God to please let my dad be there. He is the main reason that I was in Dubuque for all this time in the first place. He will save the day; I have faith in Dad. We came too far to give up now. I convince myself he could talk Mom into changing her mind once he got to talk to her. Grace drops me off at Grandma's. It is a very long and sad goodbye. I think that Grace is just as hurt as I am. I credit her for being the only one who tried to change things for the better.

Grace and the crew don't stick around for long. I make my way into Grandma's house without saying a word with the intention of finding Dad. I look in the attic, bedroom, basement, and everywhere else but no Dad. I bet that he is in the woods with Sissy. We have a hiding place called Dead Man's Cave where we like to explore. I thought maybe he is just hanging out there, so I still have hope. I make my way to the cave, but he was nowhere to be found. I got a sick feeling about the whole situation.

I barely got into the house when I hear a car pull up. I turn to see who it was, and to my disgust, it is Tyrone. The beast with a big fake grin on his face is sitting behind the wheel of the blue Rambler. Mom, on the other hand, looks excited to see me. Even though I know I must go back, I am glad to see my mom. It is painfully apparent that I am only minutes away from heading back to Rockford. I say my goodbyes to my grandparents as best as I can. As I hug Grandpa goodbye, I can feel Tyrone standing behind me. I feel very uncomfortable expressing how I really feel with him standing there. If I say something he does not like, I will have to answer for it later.

In the Eye of the Storm

Within moments we are loaded up in the Rambler and heading east for Rockford. As we cross the Mississippi River, I can smell the aroma of baked bread from the bakery just below the bridge. Little did I know that a long time would pass before I experienced that again.

Mom asks Toots and then me what we did all summer. When it is my turn, I talk about all the fun that I had with Grace, the girls, and Grandma.

While I am telling my story, Tyrone interrupts me and says, "I am your father, and we are a family. All the kids are going to be raised together. Get used to it. I am in your life from now on — not your people in Dubuque. Do you understand?"

"Yeah, I do." This person who is a poor excuse of a man may be a father to his two sons, but he will never be my father. My father is in Dubuque, devastated and crushed by alcohol.

My Escape

After we got home and settled in, I spent the last few weeks of the summer hanging out with my friends in Jane Addams. During this time, what Tyrone said to me in the car really stuck to me, and I decided I needed to make the best of the situation. After all, my mom, sister, and four brothers are together. I totally gave up on Dad getting me out of the situation. I love my mom, and for her I can and will try my hardest to just get along with Tyrone, but he will never take the place of my dad.

During the first couple weeks of school, Tyrone was treating me like never before. He seemed like he cared about me and wanted to patch things up like I wanted to. Mom was cool, too. It was almost like in the good old days when Mom and Dad were together and everything seemed perfect.

As time went on, I was committed more than ever to make this thing work. I often thought about what life in Dubuque would have been like if I had been adopted. I realize that I have a lot of catching up to do with my siblings. I especially missed my closest friends Barry, Mark, and Tracey.

Mark is three years older than me. I really look up to him. He is the natural leader of the group. He is tough but not a bully. In fact, he is nice unless you really do something to him or Tracey. He is one of the tallest and skinniest kids in the hood. On a rare occasion when he would get into a fight, an uncommon rage would reveal itself. He was like a man possessed. I was just glad he was my friend and not my enemy

He was from a broken family, too, though he didn't seem to be affected by it, or at least not around me. He looks nothing like his sister. She has a light complexion with the face of an angel. She has light eyes and long, beautiful black hair. I have a crush on her. She looks like Diana Ross only younger. I spend most of my free time with the three of them—free time being when I am not on lock down or away at school.

Mark and I spend a lot of time across from Nelson Park down in the backwater of the Rock River. I love to catch crawdads or just swim. Mark, Barry, Lisa, and the other kids I hung around with are from broken families. If they have a mom and dad, it is the exception and not the rule in Jane Addams They all seem to be dealing with issues in their families, but it never affects our friendship. After all, we have each other. Nobody or nothing can ever take that away from us, no matter what.

9
A NEW DAY, A NEW HOPE

Mrs. Miller is my fourth-grade teacher. She is an elderly lady with funny black glasses, long silver hair, and a big nose. She was always very serious. Ever since the first day of school, she just seems like she didn't want to be there.

I, on the other hand, very much want to be at school. Because I know being at school I am learning, but more than that I am away from them. If I do what I need to do in the classroom, I can stay in Mrs. Miller's good graces if there is such a thing.

Tyrone has told Mom and us kids on several occasions, "I am a 100 percent disabled veteran. I got hurt in the Navy. As a result, I am unfit to work." Wow. Unfit to work but perfectly fit to drink and drug like no tomorrow. Yep, I will take my chances in Mrs. Miller's class. I heard some stories about Mrs. Miller's teaching style and her angry outbursts. I am really kind of scared of her. In a matter of just days Mrs. Miller starts giving us homework every night. I had homework during third grade from time to time but not every day. I guess that is why a lot of kids did not care much for her.

After the first few months of having homework every day, we all thought she would back off a little but no such luck. All the kids I hung around had nicknames. I thought Mrs. Miller has earned a fitting nickname: Mrs. Miller the cornbread killer. The meaning behind the name is that she is a killjoy with her teaching style. Her classroom is run like boot camp with her yelling and uptight persona and the ridiculous homework assignments.

Surprise around the Corner

Mom had hinted to us kids that we may make a short trip to Dubuque during Thanksgiving break. This will be yet another chance for me to hopefully see Dad. I am still holding out hope that he will get his act together and get us out of this nightmare. I still want to have faith in him.

School is flying by so fast. Before I know it, Thanksgiving break is here. Mom did not disappoint. She has allowed Toots and me to travel to Dubuque via Greyhound. Once we got there, I spied Grandpa sitting in his truck with Sissy. He seems content puffing on his cigar. I am so excited to see him!

Grandpa is not much of a talker, and today is no different.

"Hi, kids."

"Hi, Grandpa," we say in unison.

"June called and said I am supposed to drop Toots off at Jane's."

"Do you mind, Grandpa?"

"No, of course not, honey." Once we arrive at Jane's, Grandpa puts the truck in park and waits for Toots to exit. She grabs her bag and with excitement in her voice, she says, "See you in a few days, Joey!"

"Okay, man! See you."

The next two days are a blur. Dad is nowhere around as usual. Between Grandma and Grace, I know they worked their contacts but with no success. It is still good to have Thanksgiving dinner with Grandma and the rest of the crew. I so love my family.

Our time in Dubuque is over too quickly, and what really sucks is that I never got to see Dad. I just feel so empty, so unfulfilled, without Dad's presence. Maybe he will show up in Rockford. My grandparents drove me down to the bus depot to join Toots for the trip home.

Once I say goodbye to my grandparents, I join her on the bus for the long ride home. Toots seems to be taking everything in stride. I, on the other hand, am having a hard time accepting the fact that I am being sent back to that hellhole. I ran to the back of the bus and grabbed the first window seat I could find. Saying goodbye is so hard. I think it was hard for my grandparents as well. With tears streaming down my face, I continued to wave bye as the bus pulled away until I could no longer see them. Here we go; I need to pull it together because I know when I get back, all the fun and games are over until next year.

10
REALITY BITES

When we get into Rockford, no one is there to pick us up.
"Toots, where do you think Ma is? Do you think they forgot about us?"

"No, we will just wait. Maybe they got caught in traffic."

After one hour, the nice lady behind the counter comes up to Toots.

"Hi, Honey, do you need to use the phone to call your folks?"

"Yes, please. I don't know what happened to them." The lady escorts us behind the counter to call home. I can hear Toots talking to Uncle Ronnie.

"We are at the bus station waiting for Mom to come get us. Do you know where she could be?"

"I don't know. She left with Tyrone over two hours ago."

"Doesn't she know we are coming home today?"

"They said they were picking you up, they just didn't say when. They are at a birthday party at the Elks, maybe they are down there."

"Okay, man, if they come home, tell them we are at the bus station."

"I would come and get you guys, but I am babysitting your brothers. Talk to you soon."

Great, I thought, *here we are, stranded once again, waiting around and not knowing when they would show up.*

Just as we make our way back to the waiting area, Mom makes her grand entrance in all her drunken glory, staggering into the waiting area with Tyrone close behind. I am so embarrassed by their drunkenness, I pretend not to hear Ma calling my name "Joey, come on! I got the car running, got to get you kids home!" No hi or how was your time in Dubuque, how are you doing—nothing.

Toots and I follow them to the car and load up. As Tyrone drives us home, I begin to think about my brothers. I really miss them. It has only been a few days that I have been away, but I can't wait to see them. Marty, Greg, Leon, and Andre all came barging out of the apartment rushing toward Toots and me as we exit the car. They all look so much bigger than I remember. They are such a sight for sore eyes. I love my brothers.

Weekend of Bliss

A few weeks later Mom plays her trump card. She comes running upstairs into our bedroom.
"Joey, Joey," she shouts waking me up.
"What's wrong, Mom?" Silence. I sat up in my bed looking on as she begins rummaging through all the dresser drawers. I build up the courage and ask, "What's going on, Ma?"
"Just get some decent clothes on—we are leaving!"
"Leaving? We're leaving?" Could it be Ma had enough of the treatment she was getting from Tyrone? Whatever the cause of her decision, I am ready to get the hell out of here. By the time, I got dressed, Toots has gotten all the boys dressed and fed. When I run downstairs, I see Mom walking out the door with the kids behind her. I run out the door to catch up to them. My heart is pounding so hard I think it's going to come right out of my chest.

I am worried Tyrone will come home just as we are making our escape. Ma must sense that, too. She has urgency about herself that I have not seen in a long time. Maybe she thinks it is now or never. Once I caught up to them, I follow Toots who is behind Mom. Mom has Marty in one hand and Greg in the other. I pick up Leon. His little legs can't keep up with the pace. Toots is carrying Andre close to her chest. He is visibly upset. Being only two years old, he has no idea what was taking place. Leon is an armful. He was a chubby three-year-old, a ball of energy.

I look over to Toots and say, "Our great escape is on foot? Unbelievable."

"I know, man! I don't think Mom knows what to do or where to go. Tyrone will catch us for sure if we don't get off the street!"

Before long, we are traveling east on State Street for a few blocks. I know this area well. The Faust Hotel was on the left side of the street and directly across from it is the Midway Theater. Twice a year we would come up here with all our friends and sit either in front of the Midway or across the street in front of the Faust. This was because we felt this was the best place to be during the parade. I knew from experience that if we sat close to the beginning of the parade route, we all had a good chance of getting some candy that is thrown into the crowd.

Once the parade started, all of us kids would be in a free-for-all once the candy was flying. Only the fastest, most determined kids got the most candy. That was never me. I am not the fastest, strongest, most-aggressive kid, but it always worked out, and by the time the parade had completely passed our little area, I had loads of candy and that's all that mattered.

Some of the smaller kids that were sitting next to us were always too late to the party. I felt sorry for them, so I would give them some of my candy. I thought it was the best thing to do.

By this point on our journey, we are walking by the Midway Theater. I have been inside of it only once. Back in the summer, Mom and Tyrone allowed me and Toots to go see the movie *Jaws* with Jimmy and Barry. I had stashed my earnings from the Sandwich Factory. The movie was $1.50. That was a lot of money, but it is worth every penny.

I am with my sister and two of my best friends. Barry had been my friend from day one of living in the projects. He was a very loyal friend. Jimmy was a good friend as well. I didn't trust him as much as I did Barry, but he was a lot of fun to be around. The movie was awesome. It centered on a killer great white shark. Some of the scenes in the movie were scary, but I managed to get through it. I guess for that reason, going there to see such an epic movie at the Midway, a very old building with such great history has a special place in my heart

Ma is a woman on a mission. She is acting very nervous. I mean I am accustomed to her smoking, but now she is chain smoking, I mean she must have set a record for the number of squares smoked in a period of five minutes. I am nervous as well. I am happy as hell to be free from Tyrone, but there is no time to celebrate yet; all doesn't seem quite right for my liking.

"Here we are," Ma proclaims nervously.

"I am going to check us in. Toots, you and Joey keep an eye on the boys. I'll be right back." The Imperial 400 Motel is our new home — give me a break!

It is a three-story motel right next to the Midway. There is a huge neon sign in the front with a blinking smaller sign below; it is blinking obnoxiously nonstop "vacancies."' The Imperial 400 is in the heart of downtown. It is an eyesore, in my humble opinion, a yellow brick three-story building that looked newer. The eyesore is all the hobos sleeping next to the dumpsters in the back of the parking lot, not to mention all the hookers working the block. It is kind of a scary place. Why did Mom bring us here of all places? She has a sister in town. Why didn't she call Alice? We had our share of streetwalkers around the projects. They never bother me, but I really hate it when I would return home after working at the Sandwich Factory. There is an alley that ran behind the business all the way to Division. Park It Market sits in front of this alley. This is where I go to buy candy. It is also the place where hobos buy their booze and hookers prowl around.

One morning as I am walking home, I look to my left down the alley. There in plain sight is a hooker servicing a man. This type of thing is all too often in the projects. For that reason, when I see all the prostitutes milling around the motel, it leaves a sick feeling in my stomach.

During the holidays and whenever there was a parade, it seems to me that all the hobos and hookers scatter like roaches. The powers that be didn't want the epidemic around during those times. Likewise, the hobos and hookers didn't want any unwanted attention from the police, I am sure. There are always cops patrolling the area on foot during parades and other events. I guess out of sight, out of mind.

Free as a Bird with a Broken Wing

Once Ma gets us checked in, the clerk show us to our room. The place is tiny, but it is away from Tyrone. That's all that matters, home sweet home. I can deal with this.

"Joey and Greg, unpack the bags and keep an eye on the other kids. Toots is going to the grocery store with me to pick up some food."

"What are we supposed to do after we get the bags unpacked?"

"Have the kids watch TV. Just don't go outside," she snaps.

"Joey, why are we here?" Marty asks through his tears.

"Ma and Tyrone have been fighting a lot lately. Maybe she got brave and decided enough is enough. It's okay, Marty. Everything will be okay," I promise. Marty is too young to understand, but he is aware things are different. It didn't take long for Ma to get back. She bought bread, lunchmeat, milk, peanut butter, and jelly. After we all ate a late dinner, we retired for the night.

I look on as Toots turns on the TV to find something for the kids to watch; the only station she can find is playing *Hee Haw*, a country music program. Within twenty minutes everyone is sleeping. I try to settle in for the night. All I keep thinking about is, *Will Tyrone find us?* I finally drift off to sleep.

The next morning, I am aroused by the noise of a blaring TV. I sit up to see Toots and the boys watching cartoons. *The Flintstones* are on, one of my favorite shows. I join in on the fun when Mom comes out of the bathroom.

"Okay, let's go kids."

'Where are we are going, Mom?"

"Down to the library. Get your shoes on."

"Can I get some breakfast first?"

"It's all gone," Greg says.

I want to say, "That's just great," but I don't want to get on Mom's bad side. Marty turns off the TV and leads the way out of the motel room. We mill around downtown, hoping to get a bite to eat somewhere inexpensive when out of the blue, there is my dad standing at an intersection preparing to cross. I think I am the first to catch a glimpse of him.

At first, I think my eyes are playing tricks on me. As he crosses the street opposite of us heading west, I am studying him closely. He is walking with his head down, unaware of our presence. Ma and the crew continue to forge ahead, but I decide to investigate this more. I see him in my dreams every night.

"Dad, is that you?" I say to myself.

"Dad, Dad!" I holler across the way.

"It's me, Joey!"

"Joey, hey, what are you doing?" he says with a strange look on his face. Is he as happy to see me as I am to see him?

As he begins to make his way over to where I am standing, I holler to Toots, "Toots, stop. Dad is here!"

I watch to see if she is paying attention to what I just said. Ma stops dead in her tracks and makes a beeline back to me.

"Your dad isn't here; he is out hopping freight cars somewhere. Now get your crap together and—" Before she could continue to ride me, my dad arrives on the scene.

"Hi, June," Dad exclaims with a huge smile on his face. She turns ten shades of white when she hears his voice over her shoulder.

11
ONLY DREAMING

I am awakened by Mom shaking my shoulder. I roll over onto my back. She is standing directly over me.

"You need to get up!" *It was just a dream*? It was just a dream! I am so sad I want to cry. It seemed so real! Once I get my bearings, I mill around the room. The boys are watching TV, oblivious to anything around them. Mom calls me to the front door.

"Joey, I need to go get some milk and donuts. Help your sister get the boys dressed." She hollers with that dragon cigarette breath.

"Okay." I don't even see Toots.

"Marty, where is Toots?"

"She is in the bathroom."

"Oh, okay,"

I join the boys in front of the raggedy TV. I get lost in the show *Fat Albert*. Toots finally exits the bathroom. She looks like she has been crying.

"Are you okay, man?"

"No! Where is Mom?"

"She went to get some food."

"Okay. I have a feeling she is going to take us back to Tyrone. I mean she has not really tried to ask anyone for help—not her family or even the police. I don't understand her logic."

"I don't either. We better get the kids dressed. I don't want her mad at me when she returns!" Toots and I round up the boys in the bathroom. The bathroom is really disgusting. The tub, toilet, and sink have stains in them. It looks like the bathroom has not been cleaned in a long time. We just must deal with it. There is no other choice at this point. We put Andre and Leon in the tub first, followed by Marty and Greg.

"I want to take a bath by myself," Greg shouts.

"I know you do, but we have to be ready when Mom gets back. I think she is going to take us somewhere cool."

"Alright," he says. We just finished getting the boys dressed when Mom returns. I am hoping she has good news. Perhaps she has figured out her next move. I have my fingers crossed. Mom returns with a half-gallon of milk and a dozen donuts. We inhale the food in no time. We have been surviving on peanut butter and jelly sandwiches, so this was a nice treat.

After everyone ate, Mom broke the silence "We are going to the library, kids."

"Cool. I have never been there, Mom," Greg says.

"It is really nice, and there is a section for the kids to play." Mom puts Leon and Andre in the stroller and leads the way out of the room onto the sidewalk. She is looking a little more relaxed this morning. Maybe she has got a plan, finally.

We cross the State Street Bridge and head north. Mom leads north on Whitman toward the library. Toots and I have been there with the kids from the Center on a recent field trip. I love the library. Marty and Greg are so excited. They have never been there before. I am just hoping once we get there, they will like it as much as I do. They can't read yet, but Marty loves to draw. He draws a lot. I think he is talented for his age. Greg is not artistic. I think he just wants to see what cool toys they have in the playroom.

Once we get to the library, to my utter shock, Mom allows Toots and me to do our own thing.

"You guys need to be back here in one hour," Mom says. It is big, with so much stuff to do. I really feel like a normal kid when I get to spend time here. Toots likes it even more than me. She just loses herself with all the cool stuff. I didn't like to read much, but that's what a library is there for, and she took full advantage whenever she could. She is having a field day. Going all over the place,

I can't keep up with her. I decide to go to the playroom with the boys. Toots reappears sometime later.

"Are you ready to go?"

"Yes, let's go, man." When we got to the main entrance, we can't find Mom.

"Joey, you check around here, and I'll check the bathrooms."

"Okay, hurry up." I survey the main floor looking for her, and just as I give up hope, I see her. She is sitting over at a phone booth with tears streaming down her face. I am not sure who she is talking to, but she is sure upset. I go back to find Toots.

"I found Ma, man. She is using the pay phone by the main entrance."

"Okay, let's go over there, so we can leave"

As we head in that direction, Ma meets us halfway.

"You kids ready for some lunch?"

"We're starving, Ma," Toots replies. With that, Mom sets off to yet some other unknown destination. Ma seems to be feeling better than she did a short time ago. I wonder who she was talking to. Was it Tyrone, one of her sisters in Dubuque, or maybe Dad, but I doubt it. I need to find out. It bothers me to see her in the condition she was in before, and I don't like it because when she gets that way, the drinking is sure to follow. Although our living situation has changed, I don't think that will ever change with her.

We find a fast-food joint just down from the library. Once we got to the place, Mom orders a bunch of hamburgers and fries to go. With the food in hand, we walk to a little park and have a quick lunch. Mom is very nervous. She is not eating. I guess she is too on edge. After lunch, we go back to the hotel for what I thought was going to be another night at the roach-infested dump, but I am wrong, dead wrong.

12
STRANGER AT THE DOOR

The next morning there was a knock on the door. *Who could that be?* I thought. Toots opened the door to my biggest fear. Tyrone!

"Hey, come here and give me a hug." The boys ran over to where he plants himself on the bed. Toots and I stayed out of the way. I would give a million bucks if I knew what was going on in Toot's head. She was just standing there, not saying a word. She looked as crushed as I was. After all the greetings were out of the way and all our possessions were packed into the car, we were off once again into the trenches.

Later that night after we had dinner, Tyrone allowed Toots and me to go to the Center, where our friends were sure to be found. I ran from the house in break-neck speed, relieved to be further away from that messy, so-called family. My friends seemed to know things were rocky at home. I never talked about it. How I wished I could tell someone in hopes of things turning around. I was afraid of the consequences if I opened my mouth. Whenever I would go to the Center by myself or with my kid brothers, I would play all the different games and other activities, which helped me take my mind off all the crap at home. Tonight was different, though.

"Joey, where have you been?" Mark shouts across the Center. The place is packed. I don't see any of my other friends. In fact, I don't know where Toots went. I walk over to Mark who is standing in front of the bumper pool table. He gives me a hug and says, "Want to play?"

"Sure." I watch on as Mark gets the games started. I didn't answer his question about where I have been because I don't want people to know. I can't relax. Whenever I hear someone coming into the Center, I tense up, thinking Tyrone is coming to get me. Apparently, Mark can tell I am not myself.

"Joey, are you okay? You keep looking over your shoulder like someone is after you. What's up?"

"I will tell you after our game." I was rehearsing in my head what I was going to tell him. I trusted Mark.

I could never beat Mark at bumper pool. Tonight was no different. After we finished up, I walked to the front door, motioning for Mark to follow me outside. Once we were away from prying ears, I proceeded to tell him.

"Well, a few days ago, we left Tyrone. That's why you have not seen me around. I thought Mom had serious plans to take us somewhere safe. But she called him to pick us up."

"Where did you guys go?"

"The Imperial Palace."

"That place was scary, man. Well, are you guys going to be okay?"

"I don't know, man. Please don't tell anyone, Mark."

"I won't."

"I don't know, just hope things get better soon!"

"Me too, Joey."

I hung out until 8:00 p.m. and then headed home. I purposely took my time walking. I was in no hurry to get back to the trenches. I got home just under the wire. I was not surprised to see Ma drinking a beer with Tyrone in the kitchen. I tensed up as I walked into the living room. I really didn't know what to expect from them. I joined my siblings to watch TV. As the night progressed, I couldn't relax. I walked over to Toots and whispered in her ear.

"I am going to bed."

"Okay see you in the morning."

I woke up to the sound of the bathtub filling up with water. Perhaps Toots was going to take a bath. I walked into the hallway to see if indeed it was her. That's when I saw Mom smoking a cancer stick and drinking a beer

She was filling the tub with scalding hot water. Steam from the water was engulfing the room.

"Hi, Mom. Are you taking a bath?"

"No, you are! I hate you. It is all your fault. I have tried to keep the peace with Tyrone but he continues to beat me because of you!" she stopped speaking to take another drink.

"Toots, help!" I hollered into the hall, hoping Toots would show up and settle Ma down, but no Toots. Next thing I knew, Ma picked me up and threw me into the tub.

"Maybe this will teach you to shut your mouth!" she screamed.

"AAAHHHH!" I tried to fight my way out of the tub, but she was too strong. The water was unbearably hot. I was about to give up fighting when Tyrone stormed into the bathroom and yanked me out of the tub.

"*What in the hell are you doin', June?*" Ma had the strangest look on her face.

"What is it to you, ape! This is my kid, and I'll handle this *my way*."

"No, you won't, June. You need to take your butt to bed. Joey, are you okay?"

"No, I am far from being okay…"

"Go to your room and get changed. Don't worry about your Ma; I will put her to bed." I was not in my room more than thirty seconds when Ma barged into the room. *Not again,* I thought. I scurried under the bed where she couldn't get to me — in my hiding spot.

"Get out here, you little creep. I'm not done with you yet. She was screaming so loud that Toots finally came upstairs to see what was going on. She came into my room, trying to settle Mom down. Mom turned her attention on Toots and began to beat her mercilessly. I could hear Tyrone as he made his way up the stairs. He ran into my room and pulled Ma off Toots.

"June, *leave these here kids be*! *Go to bed*! I watched intently as Tyrone dragged Ma to her room by her arm. When I knew Tyrone had Mom under control, I quickly crawled from under the bed and ran as fast as I could down the stairs. I knew from experience

Tyrone can turn on me on a dime. His disdain can go from Mom to me in a heartbeat.

I loved my Ma, but she acted like she hated me. What did I do? God, please help me! I really didn't have any lasting injuries from the "fun bathtime experience"—at least not physical. Toots was standing above the kitchen sink. Her nose was bleeding profusely.

"What can I do to help, man?"

"Nothing; just leave me alone," she managed through her tears. I trudged back upstairs. I ripped off my wet pajamas and put on a clean set. I was being as quiet as I can. I didn't want any more surprises tonight. I climbed into bed and cried myself to sleep.

13
TOOLS OF THE TRADE

Sunday morning, Toots woke me up for breakfast. When I joined everyone in the kitchen, they were already eating. Mom did not cook breakfast during the week. This was a treat I could never get enough of. As we ate together, I was hoping she would apologize for last night, but there was no sorry, no "I was drunk; I didn't mean to hurt you." Nothing, not one word. She didn't care. Who was I kidding? One thing was for sure; I couldn't trust her anymore. I was having doubts as to why I was brought back here from Dubuque. I didn't think love had anything to do with it.

I was really struggling with school. Fourth grade was so much harder than third grade. At least I had Good Grooming.

Good Grooming (G.G.) had always been fun. I dread leaving there after our time was up every Tuesday evening. I volunteered whenever possible to stay behind to help clean up. The leaders asked for kids to help all the time, but not many kids were eager to help. I saw this as an opportunity to stay away from home just that much longer. My plan had problems from the beginning, though. Ma and Tyrone instructed me to report directly home after G.G. I decided if I could impress the staff at G.G., they would request my presence and I would be in like Flynn.

Mary and I cleaned up the Center in a short time. Afterward, as she escorted me to the door so she could lock up for the night, I asked, "Mary, can I stick around to help next time?"

"Actually, Joey, we encourage the other kids to help as well, so it would not be fair if I allowed you to continue to help in this manner." My heart sank to my feet. My plan was already doomed. *No way*, I thought, *I will not let this golden opportunity slip through my fingers.*

"Please, if I don't do a good job, you can fire me, and I will never ask again. Besides, no one else ever wants to stick around to clean. I won't let you down, I promise!"

"Well, okay. I will need you to stick around after the next session; we will do a better clean up, so just know it will take up more of your time."

"That's okay; I will just need to get permission from my Ma."

"I will send a request form with you to give her to fill out; that way she will be fully aware of our intentions." *Thank you, God, thank you for Mary, thank you for Good Grooming, thank you for this place.* As it turned out Mom was fine with me helping at the church. I think that this whole process was a little too easy. Was Ma up to something? Was this her way of saying sorry for be so mean and hateful, have fun, and do your thing? Time will tell.

The days I went to G.G., I made sure I did an extra good job, which took extra time, but that meant being away from home. If I did well, I had longevity here.

On the days, I didn't have G.G. or Bible Club, I walked straight home to help Toots with the boys. Ma and Tyrone sure had busy lifes for neither one of them working. They were always going here, there, and nowhere in particular. For me to stay out of their way, I cleaned up around the house. I already had chores, but I liked to clean up, especially dusting. I got lost during clean-up time around the apartment. It helped time go by fast. When I was not changing diapers or tending to the other boys, I found things to do. Maybe if Ma or Tyrone saw that I was doing more than they ask of me, they would loosen up and treat me like the other kids.

Whenever I got in trouble. Tyrone had a tool of the trade he liked to use. It was the wooden paddle that Mom has had before. He drilled holes for a more lasting effect. Sometimes he used his forty-four-inch-long belt. It was one long, thick piece of leather misery. His whippings weren't like the ones Dad would dish out, a few swats to the butt. Oh no, Tyrone liked to lock me in the basement for hours before he would administer his form of punishment. He said he wanted me to think about what I did to deserve this. I thought he enjoyed that whole ordeal. In fact, when he decided the hour of judgment was at hand, he would gather everyone around to watch as he would have me bend over the stairs butt naked when he would go through his series of questions and his disappointment with me. After a point or two, he would deliver a blow.

"AAAHHH that really hurt! Please, no more, please!"

"Boy, if you move again, you get another one!"

"Okay, I'm sorry. I won't move." I tried to anticipate his swing, and I moved, thinking to myself that if I moved further away from him it would not hurt as much. I didn't think he noticed my little trick.

"Boy, do you know why you are in trouble?"

"No, I didn't do anything wrong!"

"I told you to come straight home after school on Wednesdays to babysit. Since you can't listen to simple orders, I will just beat some sense into you! Because of you, I had to cancel all my plans." Whack, Whack, I didn't see it coming, and boy, did he nail me right on the butt.

"I'm sorry, I'm sorry. I will come right after school every day if you want. Please, no more swats!"

"Who told you to move? Did I say you can sit down? Get up and assume the position!"

"No more," and with that I ran up the basement stairs like a man possessed to get away from him.

To my utter amazement, there stood Ma atop of the basement stairs, blocking my access to freedom.

"Ma, please make him stop!" She had a look about her that I had never seen before; it really scared me maybe more than Tyrone. Before I knew it, Tyrone grabbed me by the arm and threw me down the stairs where this whole thing began. I could tell he was a little upset now, but he didn't say another word. I figured he would give me an extra swat or two for my little stunt, but nothing prepared me for what happened next. I ran over to the couch to hide behind it, one of my hiding places, but that plan backfired. He grabbed me by the arm and lifted me into the air up to his face.

"Don't you ever try to run away from me again, do you hear me?" Before I could even respond, he began to slap me on the back of the head, repeating the same question. Both Tyrone and Mom were heavy-handed toward me. They were smart, though. Whenever they would leave a visible mark I was not allowed to go to school or hang around outside. That was until the evidence went away. The deal was if there was a report of child abuse, it wouldn't fair well for those two. We kids will be taken away, and so will the financial aid they receive every month. All this meant to them was less money to get drunk and high. When Tyrone decided he was done with me, he ordered me to my room. I didn't need to be told twice, I flew up the two flights of stairs and quickly jumped under my bed. I would hide here when I thought there may be trouble brewing.

Both Ma and Tyrone were nuts; they both had it out for me. Why? I had tried hard to be a good kid ever since I came back from Dubuque. Over the remainder of the school year, I really struggled with my studies. The things I really enjoyed at school seemed to be a chore. Most days, my focus was not on the daily lessons but on things at home and the reality that I had to go back to that scary place.

Lock Down

Most days when I returned from school I would find Tyrone in the living room listening to music with his friends. Mom had been working second shift, so I didn't see her much. We had only been reunited with Tyrone for two months. He continued to drink and smoke weed every day. I didn't know where he got the money for such things. We never seemed to have enough money to keep the cupboards full.

On a Wednesday I got home right after school. As I headed up to my bedroom, Tyrone yelled.

"Boy, go into the basement and watch your brothers."

"I have homework. I was going to my bedroom to get it done." He stood to his feet and walked to the bottom of the stairs. I could see he was upset. He had his right hand in a fist as he began to grind his teeth. His jaw muscles were working overtime. I looked over at his friends. They were looking on as if to say, "Boy, you better do what he says."

"You got the count of three to get your butt into the basement!" he screamed. I made haste into the basement. I could see all the boys playing with the few toys we had. They seemed so content.

This became the pattern every day. Tyrone sent us to the basement. When he was in a good mood, he would allow Marty, Greg, Leon, and Andre upstairs with him and Toots. I was left to my own devices. I guess he thought he was punishing me. Little did he know, I liked the basement. I was out of his reach.

There was a little black-and-white TV down there, so I would try to find something to watch. Usually *The Brady Bunch* was on. It was one of my favorite shows. When I watched it, I daydreamed about life with Dad.

When Ma would return home from work, one of the first things she did was to come downstairs by us. One Friday after school, I ran home. I was planning on going to the Center with friends. Tyrone met me as I walked through the front door.

"I am going to my mom's. You need to watch the boys. They are in the basement."

"Okay, is Toots here?"

"No, she is at my mom's." He turned and walked out to the car. I was wondering why he was taking the car. His mom lived less than a block away. Whatever! I made my way down to the basement. I was so upset. All my friends were at the Center, and I was stuck in the basement.

Greg was sitting in front of the TV, watching *Spiderman*. Andre and Leon were sitting on either side of him. Marty was sitting on the couch, drawing a picture of Spidey. I sat down next to Marty and asked, "How was school, Marty?"

"It was good."

"That's great! Greg, did you have a good day?"

"Yeah, man." I settled in and watched TV with the boys for an hour or so. I didn't know what was taking Tyrone so long, but I was getting hungry.

"Joey, I am hungry."

"Me, too," Greg said.

"What are we having for dinner?" Leon asked.

"We have to wait until your dad gets home, Leon. You know we will get in trouble if we leave the basement." An additional hour passed, and all the boys were starving.

"I am going to find something for us to snack on until Tyrone gets home. You guys stay here."

I was searching high and low for something, anything. I found a box of saltine crackers and headed back to the basement. Just then I heard Tyrone.

"What in the hell are you doing in the kitchen?"

"I just wanted to grab some snacks until dinner for me and the boys. We are hungry!"

"Did I tell you to come get some snacks?"

"No, no, you didn't."

"That's right! Hit it! I will be right down to deal with you!" When he said hit it, that meant you better get down those basement stairs as fast as you can and just hope that you move fast enough for his liking. I flew back downstairs and hid. I just wished I could become like the invisible man, so he couldn't find me. My brothers heard the commotion, and they knew what was coming as well. He was really ticked, and when he shows up down here, it was not going to be pretty.

Squeak! Stomp. Stomp. Tyrone was making his way down the stairs. From where I was hiding, I could see all the boys standeing at the bottom of the stairs. They eagerly greeted him as he reached the basement. When he came down here, it was usually bad news for one of us. That fact was not lost on the older boys. I was holding my breath, hoping the trouble would pass.

"Joey, get out from under those stairs, boy! What are you doing under there, anyway?"

"I don't know, just trying to stay out of the way, I guess."

"I am going to let you slide this time, but the next time you go into the kitchen without my permission, you will have hell to pay! Is that understood?"

"Yes, I understand," I replied, staring at the ground. I stood there frozen in place as Tyrone ascended the stairs. All I could think was *I understand I did nothing wrong. I understand my brothers are hungry. I was just trying to get them something to eat. I also understand Tyrone really hates me.*

14
SPLISH SPLASH

It was the third week in December, and parent-teacher conference was here. Before we left from home for school, I went upstairs to change into something clean. In my haste, I grabbed a clean shirt and pants. I couldn't find any clean underwear. So, I thought *no underwear, no problem.* I put on a clean pair of pants. As I pulled up the zipper my private part caught in the zipper OUCHHHHHH. I never felt such pain in all of my life! After what seemed like an eternity of discomfort the pain subsided, I made my way downstairs where Ma, Toots, Marty, and Greg were waiting for me.

"What in the hell were you doing up there? I heard you jumping all around."

"Oh, I stubbed my toe." She seemed content with my answer. I took my sweet time walking to school. I was hoping Ma would make this thing as quick as possible, so I could get somewhere and try to get uncaught.

To my utter dismay and astonishment Ma took ample time, talking to all four teachers. I did not say a whole lot as we met with Mrs. Miller. The three of us were sitting at a little table going over a variety of items. Whenever one of them made a comment, I nodded my head in agreement. Although the pain had subsided to almost nothing, I knew I was still in trouble. When we finally made it home, I went upstairs to bathe and prepare for bed. I took care to undress down to just my pants. After a couple of deep breaths,

I tried to free the zipper, no luck. After all my vain efforts, I hollered for Ma.

"Ma, please come up here. I need your help!"

"What now, Joey?"

"Pleaseeeee, I need your help!" So there I was standing in the bathroom in dire straits waiting on Ma. My God! She was taking forever. If ever I needed her to rush to my aid, it was now! "Why haven't you taken a bath yet, Joey, You need to get in the tub, so other people can use it, too!"

"But, but I can't get my pants off, I got the zipper stuck down there."

"How in the hell did you manage that, you dummy? Let me see. Why didn't you wear underwear?"

"I didn't have any clean underwear."

"Stand up, I will fix this problem."

Thinking this whole thing would go smooth—wrong. With one real strong pull, she pulled the zipper up and with one motion she yanked it down.

"AAAAAHHHHHH AAAAAHHHH!"

"That will teach you not to get dressed without underwear. Now get in that tub, and take your bath and *get to bed*. With that, she walked out of the bathroom, slamming the door behind her. She didn't even ask if I was okay. I was far from it. I tried to get the bleeding to stop, all the while wondering why she was so brutal toward me. I made a mistake, but to her it was much more. I slid into the tub after the initial pain subsided. By this time, the water was lukewarm, but it felt soothing.

15
A HOUSE IS NOT A HOME

Mom had been working at Eclipse full-time recently. Tyrone did not work. He could drink and drug all the time, play basketball, and be a menace toward me. But to work and support the family was one something he was not interested in doing. For the last year or so, he had promised to move us out of the projects. He had made lofty promises for years. This was just another pipe dream. Boy was I wrong! By June, mom enrolled us at a school on the west side. It was then that I realized we were really moving. Maybe this change would be just what was needed. Perhaps they would start to treat me like a human.

Around 7:30 a.m. on Monday morning, Ma loaded us up in the Rambler and delivered us to the front of our new school, McIntosh. As she pulled the wagon directly in front of the school, she gave us the following directions, "You kids need to check in the office with these papers and then you will be assigned to a teacher. Go before you are late!"

We exited the car Toots, Marty, Greg, and I were standing in line outside the school office. We didn't know what to expect. Some of the kids that passed by us in the hallway looked tough. Many of them were wearing the gang colors blue and black for the Gangster Disciples. Other kids were wearing red and black, the colors of the Vice Lords. They didn't seem like they wanted to be there. They all had a mean look on their faces. I had always found school to be a place to go to escape the torture of the home life. Now that was not the case.

A few of the black kids walked by and hollered in my direction.

"Where you from, boy? What set you repping?" There were gangs in my old neighborhood. I knew how to handle myself around these sawed-off gangsters.

We lived in a rough area of town. There were boarded-up homes. Many of the businesses had bars on the windows. McIntosh was in an even rougher part of the town than what I was accustomed to. I was nervous but hopeful there would be no issues. We entered the main office and sat down. Within a few minutes, Marty and Greg were escorted to their new classes. Eventually, the secretary asked us for the paperwork on the four of us. Toots politely handed the information to her. I thought it would take some time to finish this process. Just then, a short, dark-haired lady entered the office and asked, "Are you Joey?"

"Yes, I am, Ma'am."

"My name is Mrs. Gardener; I will be your 5th-grade teacher. Can you come with me?"

"One moment, Mrs. Gardener," The secretary chimed in.

"We have a problem with the paperwork. They will have to wait until we can get this straightened out."

"Okay, see you later, Joey," Mrs. Gardener said with a smile as she exited the office."

"To complete the registration process, you need to speak with the principal."

A short time later, a frazzled lady calls us back to her desk. Once we were standing in front of her desk, she looked up and said, "Welcome to McIntosh" with the excitement of someone who had said this thousands of times like an orator retelling an epic tale of a great warrior.

"Hi, thanks!" was my quick response.

"Are your parents here with you two?"

"No," Toots said, "Ma dropped us off."

"We need a parent or guardian to complete today's process! Can you call someone?"

"I will call home," Toots blurted out. The lady with the funny black glasses walked Toots over to the phone. Toots and I began to laugh in unison. This lady's glasses were so odd looking. They came up to a point on each side, sitting awkwardly on her nose. It was almost like she was wearing a little child's glasses.

I strained to hear the conversation she was having with someone on the other end, but I was too far away to figure what was being said. Toots hung up and came over by me and sat down without saying a word.

"Who did you talk to, Toots? How long do we have to sit here?"

"Tyrone is on his way, Joey. He should be here in a few minutes." A few minutes. Ha. He was as slow as a sloth climbing a tree. It would probably be more like a few hours.

As we patiently waited for Tyrone, a sharply dressed black woman walked into the office "Hello, children. My name is Mrs. Price. I am the assistant principal. Welcome to McIntosh!"

"Thanks," we said.

"I understand you are waiting for your dad, so when he gets here, we will finish the process. Thanks for being so patient." As she continued to make small talk with Toots and me, from the corner of my eye I saw Tyrone making his grand appearance. *Dramatic as usual*, I thought to myself. He walked up to where we were sitting. He greeted Mrs. Price with his Darth Vader-like voice.

"Hello, I am Tyrone, their father. Sorry about the wait."

"That's fine. Follow me, you three. We can go into my office and complete the final steps." After Tyrone filled out a bunch of paperwork, she gave us a tour of the school. It was cool. Everything was on one floor with the library right in the middle of everything. It was so different from what I was used to at Kishwaukee.

After the tour, Tyrone said his goodbyes, and Mrs. Price walked us to the cafeteria where we were served lunch with all the other kids. After lunch, Mrs. Price introduced me to my new teacher, Mrs. Gardener.

"We have already met," Mrs. Gardener replied.

"That is wonderful. Well then, Joey, welcome again." I looked on as she walked off. I couldn't help but compare my first impressions of Mrs. Gardener with that of my fourth-grade teacher Mrs.

Miller. She couldn't be as mean as Mrs. Miller, could she? After the niceties, I joined her classroom for the second half of the day. We spent the afternoon getting to know each other by sharing where we lived, what were some of our hobbies, and so on. As I sat in the big classroom listening to the other kids share their stories, I was frozen with the thought of speaking in public in front of all these kids. What will the kids think of me? Will they talk about me—the way I looked and the clothes I was wearing? I was terrified.

I felt all eyes on me.

"Joey," said Mrs. Gardener, "It is your turn to share." I just sat there with my head down. A lot of stuff was running through my brain, but talking in front of the group was not one of them. I wish I was still as Kishwaukee. I was more comfortable there to a certain extent. Here, I didn't know a soul. After a brief time, I heard the teacher ask the next child to share. Thank God, that's over. I thought the other kids were talking about me. I could hear snickering and laughing.

At the end of the school day, Mrs. Gardener pulled me aside by myself and gave me a little pep talk.

"Joey, we are happy to have you here. I have big plans for our class this year. I want you to be an active participant, okay?"

"Okay...I guess so," I responded.

Ma gave us instructions to wait for her at the front door of the school right at 3:00 p.m. I was running a little late, due to the powwow. When I got out front, there was Toots and my brothers already sitting in the Rambler with Ma behind the wheel, honking the horn like a mad woman.

"Joey, where in the hell have you been? I told you be out here at 3:00 p.m. sharp!"

"The teacher was talking to me about some things."

"Great, the first day of school, and you are already in trouble with the teacher. Wait until Tyrone finds out!"

"I didn't get in trouble. She just wanted me to feel welcome and a part of her class."

"Whatever, just shut up and get in the car!" I sat in the car without saying a word. I was excited about getting home, so I could see my friends. I discovered things did not look so good for me.

Once we got home, I headed straight for the Center in the hopes of finding Mark there.

"Where in the hell do you think you going?" Ma screamed as she stormed up to me.

"You said I could go to the Center after school."

"That was before you got in trouble at school. Get in the house and help out with your brothers!" I didn't get in trouble, but there was no sense in saying a word. She didn't believe a thing I say anymore.

I made my way upstairs to help Toots with the boys. Once I saw she had things controlled, I made it to my room to lay low. That didn't last for long as Ma came up and ordered me to work on packing some of my brothers' things for our big move. I had all my stuff packed with the exception of some clothes, of course. I wasted no time boxing up the stuff Ma had in piles on the bed. I figured if I did a good job and did it quickly, Ma would forget and I would be off the hook. I felt like a prisoner in this place. Why did she hate me so? Just as Ma predicted Tyrone was not happy about her report on my first day at school.

"Joey, get down here right now!" he bellowed up the stairs. I instinctively thought to put on some extra padding, but I could hear Ma coming up the stairs. I ran down the stairs right past her without looking at her. I said under my breath: "It's because of you I am trouble with him. I didn't do anything wrong...nothing!

Tyrone was sitting at the table making out the household bills as I walked into the kitchen. He didn't even look up from his work." Take a seat!" he ordered as he pointed to the chair directly across from him. I was a nervous wreck worried about what was coming down the pike.

"I want to know what happened today at school and the truth this time!" He yelled as he looked right through me.

"Nothing happened at school."

"So why were you held by your teacher?"

"She just wanted me to know I am a part of her class, and she wanted me to relax and open up a little."

"That's it?"

"Yes."

"Okay, you can go! Get out of my face!"

"Can I go to the Center?"

"Sure; be back here by 7:00." It was miracle—no punishment, no spanking. Thank God.

Everybody at the Center was watching a movie. It was a lot of fun just hanging out. I spent that time telling my friend Vince about my new school and how different it was. We had a great time, but 7:00 p.m. was here too fast and I had to head home. I didn't want to be late.

16
SISSY TEST

The following weekend, we finished moving out of the projects and into our new home. It was a far cry from where we lived, our Beverly Hills, so to speak. After we got settled, after a day or two, some of the neighborhood kids came over to meet us. Toots and I were babysitting the boys when there was a knock on the door. I was sitting at the bottom of the stairs as all the boys joined Toots at the door. There must have been a dozen kids hovering over her, asking her this and that. I stayed out of sight. I heard her call me to come up to meet the kids. I was paralyzed with fear. What will they think of me? Would they pick on me like my parents did? Would they like me for me? *Please, Toots, don't call me up there by you guys again*, I thought to myself because I was not going up there! Sure, enough Toots hollered down again.

"Joey, the new kids want to meet you. Get up here, man!"

I decided it was time for a nap. Maybe if she thought I was sleeping, she would leave me alone. As I was lying in bed, I strained to hear their conversations. Some girl was asking about me. What grade I was in, and so forth. I just felt like I won't fit in, so why bother introducing myself?

As time went on in 5th grade, I kept to myself. Most of the other kids thought I was not cool or tough enough. On a Friday, before class started, I was in for a treat. There were a bunch of kids gathered around Macarthur's desk. He was not only one of the coolest kids at the school—he was tough. He was known to beat kids up for no reason. The other kids called him "Duke." He was going around the room, challenging kids to "Take the sissy test." I sat at my desk shaking. I was hoping he skipped me altogether. I pretended to read a book when I felt a tap on my shoulder.

"Yo, Joey, you a sissy?"

"No, I'm no sissy!"

"Oh, yeah, punk, prove it." I don't know what this test was, but I was not a sissy punk. Tyrone called me that all the time.

Before I knew it, my shirt sleeve was rolled up, and Duke was rubbing my hand with a big eraser.

"If you are a man, this won't hurt, but if you whine, you are a sissy. Which are you, boy?"

It didn't hurt really. It wasn't until I was told to go to the sink and rinse my hand off. It hurt as the water rinsed off the dry eraser. Basically, the top layer of skin was rubbed off, and when the water touched the burn, it hurt like nobody's business. I didn't let the other kids know though. I was not a sissy. I went through a lot worse. I passed their test, but I was far from okay.

Later that night, my hand was killing me. I ate dinner as fast as I could. Then took my bath first before my siblings. I figured if I could soak it, it might feel better. Boy, I was wrong. As soon as I got it wet, it just throbbed. It hurt badly, but I was afraid to tell anyone.

It wasn't long before Ma came barging into the bathroom "Joey what's taking you so long? You need to get done so the other boys... Joey what's wrong?" she asked as I sat on the toilet seat. I finished my bath a while ago. I tried to hide the pain, but she could tell something was up.

Without anything to lose, I displayed my left hand.

"What happened to your hand, Joey?" she exclaimed.

"I did the sissy test at school. They rubbed the skin off with an eraser. If you quit that means you are a sissy, and I am not a sissy."

"No, you not a sissy; you are a retard for letting those kids do that to you!"

"Well, get dressed, and I will put some black salve on it. She then covered it with a huge wrap. It will be good as new." She was so gentle. It was something I could get used to. It was feeling better the next morning. I decided to rip it off before I got to school. I didn't want anyone to think I was hurt.

Over time, I began to open somewhat with some of the neighborhood kids. I still didn't really trust anyone, but I really liked Samuel. He lived right next door. He had a sister whose name was Kim. She had already befriended Toots on our first day here.

Samuel was really into bikes. I often saw him working on his bike, either painting it or making some adjustment. I built up enough courage one day to ask him to help me with a problem with my bike. It only took Samuel seconds to decipher the problem with my bike. We hit it off right away.

"Hey, Joey, I'm going to northwest. Want to ride down with me?"

"What's northwest?"

"Never been there? It is the community center down at the end of Johnson."

"I can't leave the block. They told us we can only ride our bikes on Shelley."

"Okay, see you later." Apparently, Samuel could run free. He was several years older than me, and his folks didn't put strict rules over his head.

Toots had made friends so easy, and it is one of her friends, Alice, that I instantly had a crush on. Whenever she would say "Hi," I would clam up. I was sure my face turned red. I was just so shy, or so they thought. What did she think about me? I was a klutz, homely, and unattractive. I didn't have any self-confidence or self-worth, especially with the opposite sex. I didn't feel good enough to talk to her. It had been beaten into me that I was nothing and never will be

Maybe they were telling me the truth, and they didn't want me to waste my time on living a normal life that a young boy my age should be living. So that's why even though I thought Alice was cute and I wondered if she believed what they said about me. If she did I would be wasting my time with her

Kari and James were brother and sister who lived down the street from us. We all went to the same school. Many mornings, Kari and James walked to school with us. He was a big guy for his age, so any fears I had around other kids at school went away when he was around because he looked out for me. James quickly became my best friend in the new neighborhood. He played the guitar. He tried in vain to teach me, but I just didn't have the patience.

Although, I was slowly developing new friendships, they could never replace my friendships and loyalty I had back in the hood. It seemed like every weekend, we made a trip back to the projects. Tyrone's ma still lived there and many of my friends. I was always amped to go there. It was where I had been through so much and those guys were always there for me. I was reminded of the old statement, "You can move out of the projects, but one can't move the projects out of you." I shed a lot of blood, sweat, and tears there. For that reason, it will forever hold a special place in my heart. The projects may be an eyesore to some, but not to me. It was just the opposite.

At Gail's (Tyrone's mom) there was always plenty to talk about. Whenever we visit, we would be rushed outside to play or sent to the basement so "Grown folks can talk" as she would often say. She liked to drink alcohol, but I never saw her carry on like my folks would. In fact, there were different times when Tyrone would get drunk and really begin to pick on me for no real reason. She would put him in his place.

Up until this point no one had ever been able to rein him in when he was out of control. All the other men in the hood knew he was nuts and not to cross him when he was drinking. He was one bad dude. That's probably the thing I loved best about her. She saved me on many occasions, and she knew I loved her for protecting me the way she did. She had my back most of the time, so I knew while around her, I was somewhat safe. When we were not making trips to the old hood, many of his no-account friends would come to the new place. It seemed once we moved into a nice neighborhood, everyone from the hood were at the new spot. I didn't realize they had so many friends. It seemed odd to me. I can remember when we were in real need of basic things while living in the projects. At those times, these people were not around. Seems to me that now that we have a little something, they all want a piece!

17
GOING NOWHERE FAST

Throughout the first year, nothing really changed in the dynamics of the family. We just were residing at a different street number. My ill treatment at their hands intensified.

After several months, I finally felt comfortable around most of the kids in the neighborhood with the exception of the alley kids. There was a housing project behind our back yard on the other side of the alley. Auburn Manor ran east to west on Auburn Street. There were only five or six buildings. Many of kids were troublemakers. I had a sense I was heading into some big conflicts with those guys.

On one occasion, I was walking down the alley toward home after school. Three boys approached me and informed me I was trespassing. I was walking through gang territory. I knew enough to know not to get involved in the gang life that was all around.

"Yo, white boy, you got two seconds to get out of the alley. If you get caught in here again, you get a beat down." Being outnumbered, I made a beeline down the alley. I ran as fast as I could. I would normally stop when I knew I was directly behind the house, but I didn't want the kids to know where I lived. So, I ran all the way down alley and around to Shelley Drive.

This was the first encounter and hopefully the last time I go through that again.

By the time I got home, my heart was beating so fast that it was hard to settle down. Later that day, I confided in my friend

Samuel, and he told me, "Don't worry about those little punks. They are nothing!" That was easy for him to say. It was not him it happened to.

I was outnumbered, and I decided to not go that way home anymore. Why put myself in a bad situation? Telling him what happened made me feel better. I didn't bother telling the folks. What good would that do, anyway? They probably thought I deserved a good beating.

All of us boys had bedrooms downstairs. When we first moved in, Marty and I were put in the smaller bedroom together. It was a cool room. It had red shag carpet and brown paneling. The other bedroom had multicolored carpet. Each square yard was a different color and the middle of the room had a sunken floor for a waterbed that we didn't have. It was cool all the same. The rest of the basement was unfinished. It had a toilet and a rec room.

It was not long before Tyrone put a TV in the rec room and informed us that we will be spending most our time down here, so we better get used to it. That was fine by me. The further I could stay away from him, the better.

Mike and Steve were brothers who went to McIntosh. From time to time I would catch a ride with them to school. They lived a few blocks away, so I would leave home a little earlier walk to their house and just wait for their dad to take us. He was real nice, never said much, but he sure liked his coffee. Anyway, Mike and Steve were identical twins. I could never tell them apart. Even when they stood side by side, I would call Mike Steve and Steve Mike. They got a kick out of it, so no harm was done.

On the way to school on a cool autumn day Steve said he wanted to talk to me about something. I didn't hang around him much. Mike was in my class. I liked him, but I could not figure out what Steve wanted to talk about.

After school the next day, I saw the brothers in front of the school waiting for their dad to pick them up.

"Hey, Joey, how is it going?"

"Fine, what's up man?"

"Mike told me you want to earn a few bucks. I am quitting my paper route, so if you think you might want to take it over, I can show you some things."

"Thanks, Steve. I think it would be a lot of fun, but when do you deliver the paper?"

"Everyday rain or shine. You will have to get up around 4:00 a.m. to put all your papers together. Don't worry; you will be fine."

I didn't know if I really wanted this job, but I knew it would be a good way to make money and help Ma with things.

That night I wanted to ask Toots what she thought about it. She always had a good insight on things, so she would give me good advice. I wanted to talk to her in private, but it seemed like she was never alone. It was killing me not knowing if I should try the job or not. I was so unsure of myself. What if I wasn't fast enough or what if I didn't take the paper to the right house? I was putting the cart before the horse. I didn't even have the job, yet I was worried about the dumbest things. I knew I couldn't ask Mom or Tyrone. I finally had a chance to talk to Toots just before I retired for the night; she was in her room.

"Hi, Toots."

"What's up, Joey? What do you want, dude?"

"Well, Steve is quitting his paperboy route, and I can take it over if I want a job. He said he would show me some things to get started."

"Do it, man. You can make a few bucks."

"I know, I just am nervous about all of the responsibilities and stuff."

"You will be alright. I will help you when I can."

"Thanks, I need to call Steve by tomorrow and let him know what I have decided. I will see you in the morning."

"Night, Joey. Don't wake me."

"Okay, I won't." I felt a lot better after talking to her. She had such a way of putting things in their proper place. After thinking more about the pros and cons, I wrote a note to myself and put it on my dresser: "Call Steve in a.m."

18
HARD CHARGER

really didn't sleep well. I had so much on my mind, and before I knew it, I could hear Marty milling around in our room. Time to get up. As was the usual routine, it was up to me and Toots to fend for ourselves and take care of the boys because Ma was just getting to bed from working the late shift. Tyrone was in no state to care for anyone, passed out drunk in his room. Once the boys were dressed and fed, I decided to call Steve. I told him I wanted the job. He gave me the number to the newspaper.

I called the number to the paper and talked to the lady in charge of bringing the papers to the house. After informing her about the change, she gave some pointers on how to collect fees from subscribers and the dos and don'ts of being a paperboy. By the tone of her voice, it sounded to me that she had given this talk hundreds of times. Steve told me before that there were always kids quitting their routes, so the paper company was always training new hires.

It was probably around 4:00 a.m. Sunday when Toots woke me up.

"Your papers are here; you need to get up and do your job dude." My job? What job? I almost forgot that I had to get up so I said, "Okay, I will be right up." I got dressed and headed outside to bring the papers inside to roll them. What happened next absolutely floored me. There was Tyrone lugging in this huge bundle of newspapers. I was in shock as I stood in front of him as he began to show both Toots and myself how to roll the papers.

"What you don't know, boy, is that I had a paper route when I was a kid. I know some things that will help you out, so get your head out of your ass and watch!" It was only seconds before all three of us were rolling up the newspapers and putting a rubber band on each roll to keep it from unrolling.

At the bottom of the bundle was a map of the route as well as the receipt book that I would need for billing the customers. There was also an invoice indicating the number of papers I should have. The Sunday paper was a real thick newspaper, stuffed with these entire store ads. I had to deliver 266 papers on Sunday and 188 papers the rest of the week. I thought to myself as I looked at the invoice: *How am I going to get these papers delivered by 6:30?*

After we got all the newspapers stuffed into the delivery bag, all three of us headed out to deliver the newspaper. I still couldn't believe not only that Tyrone was awake, but sober and helping me. What's the catch? It took all three of us to get the paper to people in time. During the route, he showed me some little things that would help me in the long run and save time as well. The load of the newspapers was quite heavy. There was a huge pocket in both the front and the back of the sack.

Tyrone and Toots were a huge help. When we got home, I could not thank them both enough for all the help. I was a little sore. Really my thankfulness was directed toward Toots. I was afraid of him. He was up to something. He never showed this much interest in me before, so I didn't go to him the rest of the day. After all, the unwritten rule was out of sight, out of mind. For me out of sight was being locked in the basement until he felt like calling me up for whatever drove him.

The next morning, I got up when the alarm went off. The clock read 4:00 a.m. Since I was on my own, I decided to use the bike. It must be quicker than walking. It was very awkward riding the bike with a huge bag over my shoulders. I quickly figured it out, and off I went. Within a few days, I found a faster route to get the papers delivered, that is, except for Sundays. I hated Sundays with a passion. Not only was it the biggest day of the week, it was the hardest. The weight of newspapers made it impossible to ride my bike. I tried several things, but the weight of the newspapers would pull me off the bike. So not only was Sunday a bigger day, it took me forever to get all the papers delivered by the deadline. Some of the residents greeted me with smiles and understanding, and there were others who were nasty. I just kept smiling because I realized I have started the process of making a difference with my situation. Over the next few weeks, I got to know many of my customers, as I would collect the fees. Many of the people were very nice, and there were a few who would tip me for all my efforts. I had always been shy, but this job helped me open up more. I realized that most people are not all bad.

As the fall season turned to winter, the job got a lot tougher. I could not ride my bike due to the snow. As a result, it took me a lot longer to get the route done. I needed help on Sundays, but I didn't dare ask Tyrone.

Things at home didn't change. In fact, things were bad, real bad. I needed to ask Mom for help. I laid awake in bed for Ma to get home from work. It was around 10:45 p.m. when I heard her come in the back door. All of us boys had a habit of greeting her upon her arrival each night, but tonight I was the only one to greet her. I heard the basement door open. I flew out of bed to greet her at the basement door.

"Hi, Ma, how was work?"

"Long and hard, dirty. I am so tired." I didn't waste any time.

"Ma can I get some help delivering the papers tomorrow?"

"If you think I'm getting up to help you, you're sadly mistaken. I worked fifty hours this week. I am beat! Ask Toots to help. Why are you waiting until the last minute to ask for help? Did you ask Tyrone?"

"I don't see you enough. Otherwise, I would have asked for your help sooner. I am afraid to ask him for anything!" Well it looks like you will be on your own tomorrow! I turned around and made my way back down stairs, crushed but not deterred.

Sunday was here so fast. I felt like I had just gotten to sleep when the alarm went off. I got dressed, ate a quick breakfast, and got the papers together. Once I set off down the driveway to begin my route, I heard the front door slam shut. I turned around to see Toots hustling out to meet me.

"Why didn't you ask me to help you, man? I didn't know you were having such a tough time!"

"I didn't want to bother you."

"I overheard you talking to Ma last night."

"Oh, I see. Thanks for helping; I really mean it." What a life-saver. We had been getting the most snowfall in decades, and all that snow really slowed me down, especially when people didn't shovel their walks. With Toot's help, it cut the time in half, and before long we were back home trying to warm up. What a way to start my day. I thought it's going to be a good day.

I got paid every two weeks from the paper, and each check was around $70, not including tips. I got into the habit of going to the local drug store where I treated myself to a Snickers bar. I also bought some items for the house, a rug or something. Mom liked coffee. I would find her a coffee cup that I thought she would like. Tyrone liked a candy called "Chicco sticks." So, I would be sure to pick up a few of those just to keep the peace with him.

It felt good to be able to earn my own money. My mom worked like a dog all the time. Why couldn't he work as well? He got a check from the VA every month, and he thought he was the reason we had a roof over our heads, but I knew the truth. Through my job as a paperboy, I got snow-shoveling jobs. I had to shovel our driveway as well. Toots and the boys would sometimes help with my customers, and then we would split the money. Usually it was just me. After a big snow, Greg and I would go door-to-door to drum up business. We would work together to get as much business as possible. We worked real fast before kids from other neighborhoods would come through with the same idea. We made a ton of money for just being little kids. Mr. Cunningham was our favorite customer. He lived across the street and down about three houses. He was a painter with a funny sense of humor. One Saturday after shoveling all day long, I made my way to One Stop Pharmacy to treat myself. Across the street and up about a block was a Ponderosa restaurant that I had always wanted to go to. Now was my chance. I had my own money. I deserved to be treated to a nice meal. Once

I made my way inside the business, I ordered a hot coco. Boy did that hit the spot. The waitress brought me a menu. I was lost in the moment. Here I was by myself at a nice restaurant buying a meal with my own money. I felt good about what I accomplished thus far. When the waitress came back I sheepishly said, "Can I have the roast beef and mashed potatoes, please?"

"You sure can, honey. Do you need something to drink with that, honey?"

"Sure, a coke, please."

I felt like a king in this place the way I was being waited on. It was nice. I felt like a normal kid for the first time in a long time.

We got a ton of snow the next day, so after church I hit all the normal spots. I was working as hard as I could to make as much money as I could to help Ma with the bills. I didn't give any to Tyrone because I felt if he wanted some money, he should work just like the rest of us. I mean he sat high on the hog, getting high all the time. He drank E.J. brandy like water every single day. Not to mention the fact, his treatment of Ma had gotten so bad. I felt I was helping by getting the family caught up the best I could with all the debts until I came home one day when I overheard Tyrone talking to Ma in the study. I stood at the top of the basement stairs and heard the all-too-familiar refrain.

"I'm gone. Make sure that boy gives you the money from all of his snow-shoveling jobs."

"Where are you off to now, Tyrone?" I heard Mom ask him.

"Central Park." With that I heard the backdoor slam shut. Central Park was the neighborhood liquor store where he got his cigarettes and booze. After I heard him go out the back door, I went to talk to Ma. I don't see her much during the week, so it was nice that she was home on the weekends. While home, it seemed to me that she preferred to spend her time with my two youngest brothers. It was so hard for me to get any real quality time with her. She still treated me like crap. I loved her no matter what. I tried to convey that by all my hard work. It never seemed to be enough though.

A little later, I had a chance to talk to Ma. She had made her way to the basement to start some laundry.

"Hey, Ma, what's new?"

"Not much, Joey," she bellowed as she started the laundry. She seemed put off by my presence, so I retired to my room and hung out with Marty. I was lying on my bed, daydreaming about Dad when I saw Marty doing something on the wall. I walked over to his side of the room where he was drawing a super hero on the wall.

"Hey Marty, don't write on the wall! You will get in big trouble!" No sooner did I get the words out of my mouth Mom barged into the room with her poison in her mouth.

"Mind your own business, bastard! Get out there and run the ringer!" I headed out to the washer when bam! I felt a hard blow to the back of my head. Mom was hot on my heels. With a cigarette hanging out of her mouth, she hollered, "It's because of you. All the beatings I have taken from Tyrone are because of you! I am done taking beatings."

I was so confused. I was doing so much to help the family and stay out of their hair.

"What did I do, Ma?"

"What did you do? What did you do? You are a daily reminder of your Dad to him and a royal pain in my ass!" She was looking rough. As we worked on the laundry, I wanted to ask her so much about maybe making a call to Dubuque to say hi to the family there. Once a month, she would call her sister Dorothy, and if she was real chatty, she would call Grandma. I could usually sense when it was a good time to pop the big question. Today is different; she seems out of sorts.

"Ma, I miss Grandma. Can we call her? I will give you money for the call."

"I will think about it, Joey. The money that you have been earning needs to go to pay some bills, so you need to hand it over." Perhaps she thought I was going to act surprised about having to give them my money. I was not. I knew it was coming.

"Sure, Ma, I want to help out. I know times are hard around here."

"Go get the money; as soon as he gets back, I will go grocery shopping." I went into my room and pulled out $56 I had stashed away. I took it out to her, hoping and praying to myself that she would not blow the money on booze. She had done this in the past.

"Thanks, Joey; go back to the ringer so we can get done." After a few more minutes of complete silence, I spoke up, "So what about it?"

"What!"

"Calling Dubuque."

"Let's get all of this laundry caught up first, and then we will call."

When I looked up to see what Ma was doing, she was nowhere in sight. Wondering where she went, I walked upstairs. There she was with a beer in her hand talking to someone on the phone. In just a very short period of time, she went from being tipsy to drunk, sitting in the study crying on the phone. I hated it when she got this way. She would get so emotional and so mean. I tried to hide when she got that way. I was resigned to the fact that I wouldn't get to make that phone call after all.

"Dorothy, he has been beating me again." She managed through her sobs. When I heard that it confirmed to me what I already knew.

I could hear Dorothy's response: "June, why don't you just leave that loser before he kills you?"

This was not the first-time Ma got drunk and poured out all her sorrows to the listener. I made my way back down stairs and finished the laundry.

I heard her wailing nonstop. I didn't know what to do. I mean if I got too close in times like these, she would grab me and wail on me. I wanted to help her, but I was afraid of her. The more things changed, the more they stayed the same. I made my way upstairs to check on her when Toots and the other boys came home through the back door. She had taken the boys to her friend's house. They had been away for a few hours. It was good to see her, a sight for sore eyes for sure.

"Toots, Ma is drunk again, and I don't know what to do!"

"Help me get the boys ready for bed. They ate dinner already, so we will get them down and then put her to bed." As we got the kids to change into their pajamas, Andre and Leon ran into the study to see Ma. I was instantly mad at her for letting herself get in this condition as well as extremely sad for the boys because they were too young to understand what was going on.

"Mama, what's wrong?" Leon asked.

"Nothing, honey, I am just tired. Give me a hug, honey." I stole a glance at Andre. His eyes were beginning to well up with tears. They didn't need to see her like this. I wanted to protect the boys from her.

Toots and I lead the boys downstairs. I went to check on Marty. He was sound asleep. Greg was the leader of the pack. As I walked back into the boy's bedroom, Greg asked.

"What happened to Ma? Why is she crying?" Before I could explain the situation, Toots injected, "She is sick right now, but she will be better tomorrow." That was good enough for him, I guess, because he rolled over and fell asleep. I stayed downstairs until I knew the boys were all sleeping, Toots headed back up the stairs to get Ma to go to bed as well. I could hear her pleading with Ma to get changed so that she could get to bed. ''It's your fault, you little tramp.''

"Whatever, Ma, you need to get to bed before Tyrone gets home. You know he will be ticked if he finds you like this!"

"Screw you, heifer; this is my house. I will go to bed when I am good and ready!" She screamed at the top of her lungs. I ran up the stairs, completely fed up with this whole situation. Mom had a hand full of Toots's hair. She hit her on her face I grabbed her before she could hit Toots again. Mom staggered backward, releasing Toots's hair. She sat down on the couch and lit a cigarette. She was staring at Toots with such hate in her eyes.

"Mom, let's go to bed," I demanded.

"Okay," she managed. I watched as she put out her cancer stick and once again got to her feet. Toots was sitting down across from Mom now. With one quick movement, Mom lunged at Toots, punching her nose.

"Aaaaahhh," Toots screamed. Blood was gushing out of her nose. She ran into the bathroom, closing the door behind her. I followed her to the restroom.

"Toots, are you okay?"

"I will be okay, man; just leave me alone." I was *so upset with Ma*. I didn't have anything else to say to her. I went downstairs. Tyrone can deal with her when he gets home. I thought he was just going to the store. That was three hours ago. I laid in my bed just crying my eyes out. Everything was such a mess. I wished I had a magic wand; I would change all of this. I heard someone walking around. I ran upstairs hoping Toots was doing better. I was worried about her. As I made my way into the study, Toots entered from the hallway.

"Toots, are you okay, man?"

"I will be okay; let's get the lush to bed, Joey."

There Ma was, in all her glory, passed out drunk on the couch with a lit cigarette in her hand. She was a small lady: four feet, eleven inches, and 100 pounds soaking wet. We had carried her to bed drunk plenty of times before, so this was not new to us. It was so sad that we must mother her all the time. Toots grabbed her shoulders, and I grabbed her feet. As we maneuvered into the bedroom, she woke and began kicking and swearing, just going nuts. We couldn't get her to bed soon enough. Finally, we got her to bed.

"I am going to bed, Toots. I have the route in the morning."

"Night, man."

I went to bed hoping to get some sleep before I had to get up at 4:00 a.m. It was now 12:00 a.m. Once I got settled in, the floodgates opened. I just hoped tomorrow brings a change for us all. I cried myself to sleep dreaming of the day this will all stop.

19
BLACKJACK

One Saturday, after delivering the newspapers, I rushed home. As I entered the kitchen, Tyrone dismissed the younger kids to the basement.

"Toots, you and Joey get your money, and we will play Blackjack. Toots gave me a look like *kiss your money goodbye*.

I *really* didn't want to play Blackjack, but I knew if I didn't I would be in trouble. He was still drunk from last night. When he was drunk, he was meaner than usual.

I went downstairs and grabbed ten bucks. When I got back upstairs, they were already playing. As I looked on, Tyrone made quick work of beating Toots and taking her money in the process. She was not so happy! "C'mon you're next, Joey." *Oh boy*, I thought, he didn't show Toot's any mercy, so I knew I already lost before I even play the game. For all I knew about the game, he could have been cheating just to take our money. That is just the way he was. This new game was a lot of fun at first, but it got ugly quick. Ten dollars was gone in a matter of minutes. Although, I could accomplish some things with my money, I felt like they were just taking advantage of me. If Ma was not asking me for money, Tyrone would take it. Chalk it up as my competitiveness or me just wanting to beat him at his own game. Either way, I was the biggest loser: No more! I decided that I was quitting the paper route. I called Trudy on Monday and informed her of my intentions. Once

Mom and Tyrone found out that I quit, they were really ticked off. I didn't care. I was looking forward to sleeping past 4 a.m. every day.

I was sound asleep when startled awake. The stereo was blaring from the living room. I walked upstairs to see what was going on. As I reached the top of the stairs, I saw Tyrone sitting at the kitchen table cleaning his beloved .38 caliber handgun. He had newspapers spread out on the table where he was feverishly working on his most precious love.

"Can you please turn the music down?" He continued to clean his gun, ignoring my request. I hung my head rejected as I made my way back to the basement.

"Wait! Have a seat!" He bellowed in his Darth Vader voice. *Oh, boy, here we go.* He walked into the living room, turning off the stereo. I began to squirm in my seat as he returned.

"Why did you quit the paper route?" I was afraid to say the wrong thing. I was studying the floor trying not to make him even more upset.

"Well, moron!" he bellowed. I have an idea. I looked in his direction. He was loading his gun. He then spun the cylinder before pushing it back into place. As he pointed the gun at my head, I could see the evil in his eyes through the dark lenses of his glasses.

"Give me one reason why I should not pull the trigger!" I once again stared at the ground, shaking violently. *Click* he pulls the trigger. Instantly I peed my pants in complete fear for my life. I jumped off the seat and ran downstairs behind the furnace as fast as I could. I heard him laughing from the top of his lungs. 'Why does he torture me like this?' A part of me wished he shot me. At least then I would finally be free!

Super Star

Spring was here. It was also the start of baseball. I had put money away to pay for the registration because this was something I really wanted to do. I felt awesome about paying my own way to play baseball with the money I earned. Mom signed me up for ball at the Center.

I had never played organized ball, but I was excited about it all the same. I had always liked baseball. I just wasn't the homerun king, nor was I a gold glove, but I loved the game.

I watched the Cubs whenever possible. I tried to emulate some of the pro guys; they were so cool. Saturday morning, Ma made breakfast for all of us kids. After my chores, she called me into her bedroom; all of us older kids have chores. However, it seemed like Tyrone and Mom put more on me than Toots, Marty, or Greg.

"Joey, I am going to take a quick shower then I'm taking you down to the Center. You need to get ready."

"I'm ready, but I don't have a glove or cleats."

"Don't worry. Tyrone has that for you; it's in the kitchen on the counter."

" What about the cleats? The paper that came in the mail said I need cleats," I asked ever so carefully.

"No cleats. You had better be content with wearing tennis shoes. Do you think we're made from money?"

The Center was clear; you need a good glove and a good pair of cleats. In the past, every glove I owned was second-hand and was usually too big and worn. Not this time; there on the kitchen counter sat a brand-new baseball glove. It looked like a million bucks, and it fit perfectly. Wow, maybe this was his way of saying sorry for being such a jerk. I didn't know. I was just ready to start to break it in. The Center was a short distance away, so it didn't take long for Ma to drive me there. My little brothers wanted to go along, but Ma made Toots stay home to babysit.

As we pulled into the lot, I noticed all the kids there to play baseball. I had to report today to be assigned a team. After we stood in line for what seemed like forever, a big man walked up to me and asked me to follow him. He took me to a bulletin board, "We have only a few openings left. I can put you on a team today. Have you ever played ball before?"

"Yes, in the projects, I played catcher!" I said matter of fact.

"No son, have you ever played organized baseball?"

"No, sir." I replied. I thought my experience from playing ball would impress him, but he was not impressed. He seemed focused on filling up all the teams' rosters so that the season could begin. I was assigned to the Orioles, and practice was to start the very next day.

I was so excited; I couldn't wait.

Once I arrived at the Center the next day, I was instructed to report to field A. I met the team for the first time. As I walked toward the field, everyone was running laps around the outfield.

"Are you here to play ball, kid?" asked one of the coaches.

"Sure am!"

"Why are you late?"

"Sorry, I got here as soon as I could." Tyrone was to pick me up from school, but he was a no-show, so I walked to the Center. I didn't tell him that because I could sense he was not accepting excuses.

"Join the other kids; you have a lot of catching up to do!"

I ran as hard as I could to catch up to the crowd. As a group, we went around the field three or four times and then returned to the dugout. As we gathered around both coaches, the mean coach hollered, "Why are you standing there? Did I tell you to stop running?"

"No, I was just following the other guys."

"The other guys were not late. Because you were late, run ten laps. Let this be a lesson for y'all. If you are late for a practice or game, you will run laps. So, what's your name again?"

"Joey."

"Okay, Joey, I need ten laps; get going." My official start of my *organized baseball* career, I liked ghetto baseball better. You didn't have to run laps. After the laps, I returned to the bench. The guys had taken the field, and the tall coach was giving fielding practice. I sat on the bench just waiting my turn to take the field or maybe batting practice, but neither happened that day. The coaches concluded practice by assigning positions to all the kids. My position was riding the bench. Not only that, but my name did not even get mentioned. The mean coach didn't say one word to me the rest of that day. The coaches concluded practice by instructing us to practice at home with our folks. The first game was in two days. I walked home rather dejected. I got off to a bad start with this team. The coach was mad at me. The other boys didn't talk to me. I really felt unwelcomed.

When I got home, Ma had already gone to work. Tyrone was in his study drinking his brandy, and I dared not to bother him. I just made a sandwich and went downstairs.

"Joey, is that you?" Tyrone hollered from the study.

"Yes, just making a peanut butter sandwich."

"After you eat, take a bath and get to bed."

"Okay, I will." I said. He didn't ask how the first day of ball went. He didn't even try to make an excuse for not picking me up at school. The little, slim hope, I had of following through with the coach's instructions dried up. I was on my own; why did I get my hopes up just to have all my dreams crushed like a bug. After my bath, Toots stopped me in the hallway.

"How did it go at Northwest, man?"

"It went okay; our first game is in a couple of days."

"Cool, you will do fine." I thought, *Yeah, sure, I am the bench warmer, real talent there.*

"Hey, Toots, think you could play with me tomorrow after school?"

"What do you need to practice for, man?"

"I don't know; the coach said we need to practice with our folks. Practice throwing and catching pretty much."

"Sure, the boys and I will play after school." Toots understood; she could tell I was down.

The next day after I got my daily chores done around the house, Toots and I played catch in the backyard for a while. She always had a way to encourage me. By game day, I was so pumped up I could not wait to take the field. After the start of the game, I realized I didn't have spot on the team. The coaches never evaluated my skills. I looked back into the stands for a familiar face, but I didn't see Toots anywhere. It was probably for the best anyway since I was not playing. For the entire season, I rode the bench with a few exceptions. When I was given the chance to play right field, it was terrible.

I about crapped my pants when a fly ball came my way during the game against the White Sox. I was playing shallow right field, and after the kid hit the ball, I retreated to catch it. Bam, the ball hit the side of my glove and dribbled away from me. The bases were loaded, and as I raced after the ball, I spied the base runner rounding first base and flying to second. I thought to myself he is a sitting duck; I could easily throw him out at second base.

As I retrieved the ball, my teammates were hollering for me to throw the ball. With all my might, I threw the ball to the cutoff man. Only problem was that it didn't even come close to him. All the bases cleared. I looked in our dugout to see the coach's eyes locked on mine. I could see him mouthing something, but I couldn't make out what he was saying. He didn't need to say a word. I was a sorry excuse for a ball player. All the fans got a good laugh out of my flaw. I prayed no one would hit the ball in my direction the rest of the game. I struggled at the plate as well. I struck out practically every time I got a chance to hit.

With school winding down for the year, I began to think a lot about spending time in Dubuque in the summer. When I received my last report card for the year, I was so confident that I passed all my classes. Tyrone knew how important it was for me to go to Dubuque each summer, and he was okay with me going if I met his standards in the classroom.

When I arrived home Tyrone was in his study as usual watching his soaps.

"Joey, where is your report card, boy?" As confident as I was prior to entering his domain, I instantly become deflated. I stood there, rifling through my book bag shaking like a leaf. He was reviewing Toot's report card as she sat on the couch watching TV. She looked so at ease, so confident. Everything came so easy for her, everything! I finally found my report card. With much trepidation, I handed it to Tyrone all the while trying to act like "No sweat, man. Dubuque here I come!" After a quick scan of my report card, he looked up at me with a look that I knew all too well.

"I am not letting you go to Dubuque, boy! You thought I was kidding? You got two Cs. That's not okay! I have a lot of things to keep you busy this summer, so forget about going there." I tried not to let him see the hurt in my eyes, but I knew he could tell I was crushed. After that exchange, I went to my bedroom. I replayed the whole situation repeatedly in my mind; I thought maybe he would change his mind as the time drew nearer. Nope! He stuck to his word.

20
BUMP IN THE NIGHT

N ow in 7th grade at Rams, I started to play the clarinet .We were instructed to practice at home as much as possible. Tyrone rented the instrument at one of the local music stores. I was excited about the whole idea. I mean really, I loved music, and this was a way I can express myself. Even more I was shocked that he even allowed me to do this, I really was. I practiced on the clarinet every night. I had a problem though. The mouthpiece had a wood reed that I would break or crack somehow while playing. This happened on a regular basis.

I thought to myself, no big deal, I have a whole pack left so if one would get a crack in it, I exchanged it. Well, this process went on for a few weeks until the day came when I ran out. I knew I need to tell Ma or Tyrone because playing it with a broken reed was awful sounding. I figured since he was the one who rented the clarinet for me, I would ask him. I thought he would understand. After school on Friday, he picked up me and Toots. Once loaded up in the car I figured I should ask him now. He seemed to be in a good mood.

"Hi Tyrone," I said excitedly.

"Can we go by the music store today?"

"For what, boy? "Well, I don't have any more reeds."

"You just got that clarinet a few weeks ago, boy. Those wood reeds are supposed to last a long time. What you are doing?"

"I am trying to play; I am trying really hard."

"I will think about it. In the meantime, just use what you got."

"Okay." I was afraid to say another word. I mean if he would take time to come listen to me play, he would realize how awful it sounded with a bad reed in the mouthpiece. I did what I could. I will just play away, and if I played long and loud enough, I will get the reeds. I could escape to a different place when I played the clarinet. The chaos that existed in this family was too much to bear. I thanked God for this opportunity

One Friday night, after drinking all day, Ma and Tyrone got into a fight. He was knocking and kicking her throughout the house. When satisfied with his handiwork, he ordered her downstairs. As I laid in my bed, frozen with fear and wondering what to do, I could hear her struggling to make it down the stairs. I decided to get up and help her. What I saw next was something I will never forget. There stood Ma at the bottom of the stairs with her shirt ripped and hanging off her. She was bleeding from the beating Tyrone had given her.

"Ma, let me help you to bed; you need some sleep" I didn't know if she was crying because she was in pain or just sad. I grabbed a washrag and cleaned her up. She was just sitting there with a blank look on her face.

"Joey, don't be surprised if I show up at school and pull you out so we can leave that ape! I mean it; I am leaving him—this time for good."

"Ma, can we talk tomorrow? You need to get to sleep." I ran into my room and grabbed a blanket and pillow off my bed. I wanted her to sleep on the sofa before she woke up the boys. She was so drunk!

After I got her settled in for the night, I went back to bed. I was laying there for a little while just wondering to myself if she meant what she said or was it the booze talking again. I finally dozed off only to be awakened to the two of them fighting in the laundry room. Before I could fully grasp what was going on, Tyrone had dragged her to the side of my bed. I was pretending to be sound asleep. I didn't move a muscle.

"Joey, Joey, wake up, boy! I want you to screw your mother. Screw your ma, boy!" I was still pretending to be asleep. Tyrone proceeded to put her in my bed. She was crying nonstop—not just crying but wailing. At this point, all the boys woke up.

"Y'all get back to bed. Don't any of you get out your beds!" Tyrone bellowed from just outside of my bedroom. I could feel his eyes on me. I was still pretending to be asleep. I could not believe what he had just said. Screw my Ma? Screw my Ma? I didn't move until I heard him make his way back upstairs.

Ma was still crying. Through her tears, she said, "Joey, I am going to die in your arms tonight." I didn't say a word, but I couldn't hold back the tears. Did he hurt her so bad that she felt like she was dying? I opened my eyes finally and give her a big hug.

"Ma, you aren't going to die, I will protect you! You are not going to die." That seemed to reassure her, and before long she was snoring away. I stayed wide awake. I was constantly checking for a heartbeat or pulse when she would stop snoring. This was the longest, hardest night of my life. He was a real-life monster. I thought monsters only existed in horror movies. Now, we were living with one. God please help. We need your help! This was the first but not the last time I experienced this nightmare.

Puppy Love

After school on Friday, I was in Toot's room just hanging out with her when I mentioned Michelle for the first time. I knew I could trust her with my secret crush.

"Joey, do you like any of the girls at school?"

"Well there is this girl in music class, Michelle. I think she is so pretty."

"I know her, man. She said she liked you, too."

"She did? When do you talk to her?"

"She is one of my friends, dude, duh." Wow, I think this might be my way to meet her, but I am just too shy.

"I am going to her house tomorrow. You should come with me; that way you can talk to her."

"I will let you know."

Big Day

Eight a.m. on Saturday morning. Toots and I wasted no time as we grabbed our bikes and rode over to Michelle's house. As it turned out, she lived close—right behind the IGA store on Auburn. Once we got there, Toots ran up to the door as I stood there by my bike. I was getting real nervous. Everything in me told me to hop on my bike and get out of there. I hoped Toots would say just the right thing to Michelle; that way she would be willing to meet me. I was frozen with fear as I looked down at my bike, not knowing what was being said between the two of them.

I heard footsteps approaching as I continued to look at my bike. I could hear more than one set, so who was it going to be? I looked up just as Michelle walked up to me. There she was with a huge smile on her face.

"Hi, Joey. How are you?"

"'Hi, Michelle, I am fine, thank you." I felt my heart beating out of my chest as we made small talk. She was more beautiful than I remember.

"Do you want to go to the park?"

"Sure, let's go," she replied with that huge smile. There was a park right across the street from her house. I pushed her on the swing for a long time, as I breathed in every word, every little quirk. She was so wonderful. I never want this day to end.

"Hey, Joey, we need to get home," Toots said as she walked up to where I was pushing Michelle on the swing.

"Really? You just got here," Michelle remarked as she jumped off the swing.

"Michelle, can I walk you home?"

"Sure, but it is only across the street, Joey."

"I know, but I want to." After I walked her up to the front door, she planted a kiss on my cheek. I blushed with her affection toward me. She grabbed my chin to face her. I considered her beautiful eyes. They were eyes that reflected care and affection for me. She leaned in and we embraced in a long wonderful kiss.

Soul Mate

I rode my bike home on cloud nine. I had my girl. Nothing else mattered. After I got home, I ate dinner and finished my chores. I called her. I bet we talked for over an hour about everything under the sun. I was so happy. Up until this point, I thought about quitting the clarinet. Now I had a new attitude about playing. I would be with my girlfriend.

21
WHEN IT RAINS, IT POURS

I planned on spending a lot of time with Michelle's family. Over the next several weeks, I spent as much time with her as possible. I didn't know why Tyrone was giving me more freedom to leave the block. After all, the rule was not to leave the street unless he okayed it. That was the rule for all of us on most days. I thought he was up to something. He had never let me branch out like this before. I had the great pleasure of spending time with her folks and sisters. They all seemed normal. If being normal means not wanting to kill each other, her parents were it.

I had a chance to talk to her dad Rod about dating his daughter. He readily gave me advice. Practically every time I was around him, he would share with me the do's and don'ts. He was very protective of Michelle. I respected that so much. Over a period of a month or so, I won Rod's favor. I could not be happier!

So now that I had her dad's blessing, I wanted to give Michelle a promise ring. It was a ring that represented my love for her. Also, it was a visible symbol of my faithfulness to her. I decided I wanted to give it to her Saturday. If it went well, I could spend the day with her. We had spent quality of time together recently, and I felt like we really understood each other.

Saturday turned out to be a real disaster.

Toots and I rode our bikes up there. I walked up to the front door to ask for Michelle. I was greeted at the front door by her dad.

"Hi, how are you?"

"I am doing okay, thanks. Is Michelle home?"

"You wait here. I will grab her." As I was waiting on the front porch, I didn't see where Toots disappeared. I figured maybe she went to the park. As I heard the screen door open, I turned to see Michelle. She looked very sad about something.

"Hi Michelle, what is wrong?"

She gave me a hug and started to weep.

"My dad is being transferred down South with his job." I was speechless as I felt the tears roll down my face. I was so focused on giving her the ring; this was such a shock. We embraced each other on the porch swing. Just then Toots came walking up to the porch. I could see her walking from the park. I didn't want her to see me like this. Thank God, Toots picked up on the awkward moment and went back to the park.

"Michelle, I will be here. I hope we can keep in touch."

"We will, Joey."

"When are you moving?" I asked with a broken heart.

"Well, we've been packing all week. We are moving on Monday. I wanted to tell you the other day after music class, but I was still coming to grips with it all." Toots showed up a little while later with Michelle's sister.

"I don't want to break you love birds up, but Joey, we need to get home."

"Okay, I will see you tomorrow after church, okay, Michelle?"

"Yes, I would like that." I jumped on my bike and rode home with Toots. Once I got home I realized I forgot to give her the promise ring. I will just give it to her tomorrow.

22
SINGING THE BLUES

Sunday was like every other Sunday. After the Joy Bus dropped us off, I ran into the house to change before I went to Michelle's. I changed quickly and went to the garage to grab my bike. I didn't know where Tyrone was, but I found Mom in the living room.

"Hey Mom, can I go to Michelle's house?"

"You better check with Tyrone. He wants you to cut the grass today." I knew if it was up to him, I would never be allowed to leave the block, let alone ride to her house. I didn't want to wait for him to show up. I rehearsed what I would say to Michelle as I cut the grass. That was the fastest I have ever got the yard work done. I had a reason for it. My girl was leaving tomorrow.

After I put the lawnmower away, I rode down past Bonnie's house when I saw Tyrone rounding the corner. I knew he saw me. He was probably wondering where I was going. At this point I didn't care. I wanted to see her one last time and give her the ring. It was my way of saying although we may be separated by mile after mile, we were still connected.

Once I arrived at the house, there was no answer at the door. I peered into the house through the window when I discovered the house was empty. There was no sign of anyone. I was devastated. She left without saying goodbye or even a phone call. I walked around back to see if anyone was outside. As I made my way to the back I was greeted by Mary, the old lady who lived next door.

"Hi, dear, no one is here. They left about an hour ago."

"Really? I thought they were not leaving until tomorrow."

"All I know is they were loading up this morning, and they came over to say goodbye."

"Did they give you their new address by chance?"

"No, dear, they didn't, why?"

"Michelle is my girlfriend; I thought we would have one more day to spend together."

"I see. I am sorry, dear. You are young. You just need to move on." *Easy for you to say*, I thought. I really cared deeply for this girl. Now she was gone. I hopped on the bike and rode home. I didn't hurry to get there. I was sad. In just a few weeks, school would be out, and I would be going to visit my family in Dubuque. I should just focus on that.

A Surprise in Store

I couldn't sleep. All I could think about was Michelle. I kept recalling everything we did together. I never thought a girl could have this effect on me. Boy, was I wrong.

At some point, I finally did fall asleep and when I woke later that morning, I could not find Ma anywhere. I went upstairs looking everywhere for her. I never thought to check the bathroom. I walked up to the bathroom door and knock three times. No answer. I pushed the door open not sure what condition I would see Mom in.

Instead of laying my eyes on Mom, what I found was Tyrone passed out. There he was completely naked, sitting on the toilet. Around him on the floor was vomit. Gross! This would not be the last time I would encounter him like this. As I walked away from the bathroom, I walked into the study where I found Ma sleeping on the sofa. She had a happy look on her face, but we all knew she was far from happy. Relieved that she was okay, I got dressed and went over to my friend Samuel's house. He was aware of some of the stuff that I had been going through but not all. He was busy rebuilding one of his bikes, something he seemed to do all the time.

"Hey, Samuel, how are you doing, man?"

"I am good, Joey, just trying to finish up with this bike so I can go waterskiing with Dad. Do you want to go?"

"I would love to man! Where do you guys go waterskiing? The Kishwaukee River or the Rock River?"

"The Rock, of course." I heard many horror stories about the Rock River, about the strong current and the huge fish. In fact, every time we would make a trip back to the projects, we would travel over the Morgan Street Bridge, which crossed the river. It was at this spot of the river that was burned in my brain. It was real fast-moving water and very dirty looking. No matter what, my friend wanted to take me skiing, so I am going. I went into the house to ask ma if I could go.

"Ma, Samuel and Oscar are going waterskiing. Can I go with them?"

"Sure, just be home before dark."

"Thanks, Ma. Thanks a bunch." What was I thinking about? Here was my Ma who was standing in front of me with a busted lip and a black eye from the night before, and I am worrying about having fun. I can't do that; I need to stick around here to make sure she really was okay.

"No, Ma. You know what, I will stick around here; maybe we can do something together if you feel like it."

"Let's see what happens Joey."

With my mind made up, I wanted to let Samuel know about my decision. I made my way back up there. I was surprised to see Tyrone talking to Oscar, Samuel's dad. I looked on as they visited. I didn't notice Samuel as he walked up to me.

"Are you ready?"

"I am not going, man."

"Is it because he is going, too? If it is, I don't really blame you."

"My mom needs some help with some things, so I am sticking around here. Thanks, anyway." With that I went back to the house. For the life of me, I could not figure out why Tyrone was going with Oscar. I knew they spend a lot of time together drinking, but I thought he didn't like the water. Oh well, I was glad about the decision I made.

Movers and Shakers

I saw Ma on the phone as I walked into the kitchen. I could smell the strong aroma of Pine Sol. Mom used this when she cleaned the house. I loved the smell but not because the house had been cleaned; it was an indication that she was in a good mood. When the Pine Sol was in the air, she was much more loving, not just to me but also to all my siblings. I was not afraid to be around her when she was in this state of mind. She was listening intently to the person on the other end. I could always tell when she was having a serious conversation. She usually paced back and forth in the kitchen, smoking a cigarette. Not now! She was sitting at the kitchen table, writing stuff down on a piece of paper. She had such a serious look of determination on her face. I sat right across the table from her, curious to find out what was going on. She continued to write on the paper, ignoring my presence. That was nothing new!

"He is here now, so I need to let you go," Ma barked into the phone. She slammed down the receiver and turned to me.

"Joey, when you go to Dubuque, you will not be coming back here. I need you to go pack all of your clothes."

"Okay, Ma, but what do you mean I am not coming back? Are you getting rid of me?"

"No, follow me to the basement; I need help switching the wash over." I followed her downstairs with so many ideas running through my head. I walked with my head down. I walked as slow as I could. When my feet hit the cold basement tile floor, I could see she was already at the washer machine lighting up a cancer stick. I was too afraid to look her in the eyes. I took my sweet time getting over to her. All that kept running through my mind was *What does this all mean*?

Game Plan

Now at the laundry room she began to lay out the game plan.

"I am putting you on the bus to Dubuque. You will be staying with your grandparents. I have had enough of Tyrone. We are leaving him for good!"

"What about Toots and the boys?"

"Toots and Marty are staying with Jane, and Greg is staying with Grace. I need you to not say a word to anyone." With huge tears in my eyes, I gave her a hug.

"I won't say a word, Ma. I promise"

As the bus rolled out of town, I began to think about all the friends I will miss. I never had a chance to say goodbye to them. I could accept that as long this plan worked out.

When I arrived in Dubuque, I wanted to see Dad. Grace and Grandma had a knack of getting in touch with him no matter where he may be.

After lunch, I helped clean up when Grandma walked up behind me at the kitchen sink. I felt her hand on my shoulder as she said, "Joey, I have not been able to get in touch with Terry. Hopefully, he will roll into town before you have to go back to Rockford." I could see the disappointment in her eyes as I turned to face her." Me, too!" I said with a grin on my face. Usually, I would be more upset about Dad not being around. I connected coming to Dubuque all these years with spending time with him. She looked at me, somewhat surprised by my reaction. Little did she know, I was in Dubuque to stay.

Now done with cleaning, it was time to take Sissy to the woods. This was our routine. I thought she was more excited than I was. Grandpa would walk her around the block or sometimes take her down by the river, but this was different for her. She could just go nuts in the woods and chase all the animals she wanted.

We spent the rest of the afternoon hanging out in the woods. On the way back home, Sissy chased a huge animal under a rock. I picked up a stick and began to jab it to flush it out. No luck, it was very feisty, putting up a fight. By this time, it began to get dark out, and I knew I was to be home by now. I was determined to get this animal.

Just as I doubled my effort I had an unexpected call. Down over the hill came Grandpa, "Joey, what you doing? You need to come in for dinner."

"Grandpa, I will be right there." I guess he was not satisfied enough with that answer. He walked down to see what I was up to.

He looked on as the creature tried to get out from under the rock. He grabbed the bloody stick.

"You need to leave this animal alone, Joey. It can bite if you are not careful."

"But Grandpa, I trapped it, and I will let it go."

"That's right, head up the hill, and get into the house." I walked up the hill just in front of him looking back a couple times to see if it ran away. It didn't move.

After dinner and my bath out of the way, I went back to the scene of the crime. I didn't see it anywhere. Where did it run off to? I was so upset. Some of my uncles hunt. I thought if I could hunt down and kill an animal, they would include me on their next hunting trip.

With the flashlight in hand, I looked high and low for that dammed beast. Just as I was about to give up the search, I heard a familiar hissing sound near a tree. I stopped in my tracks, and there to the left was the prize. It was a really big woodchuck. I could tell it was hurt badly from the blunt trauma. It was time to finish the job. I approached it, expecting it to take off. It hunched down lower to the ground, staying put. It was a sitting duck

I scanned the ground around me, looking for something to hit it with. I picked up a bowling ball-sized rock and launched it. The rock hit the animal directly on the head, killing it instantly.

The next morning Grandma had a toast party as usual. We ate peanut butter toast with jelly and drank Tang. This was my favorite breakfast, probably because she made it. I had just started to eat when Walter rolled out of bed and made his way to the kitchen. As usual he helped himself to my plate of food. Grandma hollered "Walter, I am making your food right now! Leave him be. He has a long day."

"What are you doing today, Joey?" he asked with a little grin.

"Yesterday Frank said he was taking us out to shoot his guns today."

I barely finished my sentence when Frank walked through the front door. It seemed like he was in a hurry.

"Walter, hurry up and finish your breakfast; we have plans, remember?"

"What plans, the only plans I have right now is to eat all of Joey's toast."

"We were invited to Wally's party, so we need to pick some things up on the way. I need you to hustle."

"What, what about hanging out today, Frank? I thought you were going to pick up the girls, so we could shoot your guns."

"My plans have changed, sorry," he replied unconvincingly.

I wanted to show him the animal I killed. I excused myself from the table and ran out back to gather up my prize. I timed it perfectly. He was coming out the front as I was rounding the corner.

" Hey, Frank, look what I killed. Cool, huh?" He strolled my way, giving me the weirdest look." I didn't see Grandpa standing behind me as I waited for Frank to walk over. Oh boy, I thought after I turned around and saw the look on Grandpa's face.

"Joey, I told you to leave that animal alone last night! Why did you kill it?"

"I thought Frank may want it, I guess."

"What would I do with a woodchuck?" Frank asked as he grabbed it from me.

"I just wanted to be a hunter like you, Frank, that's all." Grandpa and Frank carried the dead woodchuck back down to the woods. The look he gave me before he turned away said it all. I really blew it. Frank was not going to want to do anything with me anymore. I just wanted to be accepted by him. Up until this point, I felt like there was no real bond there.

I headed back to the attic. I was glad Grandma was not around. I was sure she would had given me an earful. I barely got upstairs when I heard some people out in the front yard. There was a window in the attic that faced the street, so I could see what was going on. I walked over to the open window, careful not to let them see me. I stood behind the heavy curtain and eavesdropped on their conversation. Grace and the girls had driven up and were talking to Frank about something. I couldn't make it out. As Frank stood outside of the driver's side door talking to Grace, I noticed the girls get out of their Ma's car and jumped into Frank's truck. I sat on the bed just crushed that I have been left out.

After a couple of minutes, I heard Frank's truck start up. I walked back to the window, and sure enough there was Frank, Walter, and the girls driving away. I guess Frank was still mad at me. I was so upset. I could feel my body tensing up. My heart was beating so fast. It felt like it was going to beat right out of my chest.

I really wanted to go with those guys. I could catch them at the top of the hill. I flew down the stairs through the living room and out the door. I ran up the hill at the intersection as fast as I could. Just as I arrived on the top of the hill, Frank drove by and waved. This whole situation taught me then and there that trying to buy someone's acceptance was just a waste of time.

I made my way back to Grandma's. I decided I was going on a bike ride. Walter had a black Schwinn that he would let me use while in town. I went up into the attic, grabbed my transistor radio and earpiece, and off I went. I usually just rode around the block as many times as I could until I was totally exhausted.

As I finished my 10th time around the block, I saw Grandma on the front stoop, waving for me to come in for lunch. I really didn't want to come in. I was just trying to work out my frustration. I mean the highlight of Grandma and Grandpa's days was Grandma going to mass at 4:00 a.m. every morning. Then she would usually shop for all the bargains. I loved my grandparents, but I didn't understand the Latin spoken at the masses; and I despised shopping, so I just wanted to do things on my own.

After I joined Grandma for lunch. I returned to riding the bike. This was one of my favorite things to do while here. The next morning, I joined everyone for breakfast. After we finished eating, we sat at the table and visited. When I saw my chance, I asked Grandpa, "Grandpa, can I ride the bike to Murphy Park?"

"Sure, just be safe!"

"I will!" I ran over to the kitchen sink and gave Grandma a big kiss on her cheek.

"See you later, Grandma!"

"Have fun, honey." I returned home an hour later to be greeted by Grandpa in the front yard with Sissy. Grandpa was sitting in the front yard in his favorite lawn chair smoking on a cigar.

"Hi, Joey, how was the bike ride?"

"It was good, thanks."

"Put the bike back in the basement, honey."

"Okay." I rode the bike to the back of the house and into the basement. As I was walking up the stairs I heard the phone ringing. Grandpa rarely answered the phone. Grandma was not around to answer it. As I made it through the kitchen, there was Grandpa on the phone "Hi, June. How are you? That's great, here is Joey."

I had not spoken to Mom since I left Rockford. I was so excited to hear her voice.

"Hi, Mom, how are you doing?"

"I am okay. Listen, I will be in Dubuque in about two weeks. I need you to start looking in the paper for a place for us to live!"

"What do you mean? I thought you had a place lined up?"

"No, so I need you to start looking, you creep! Either a two- or three-bedroom. Don't tell anyone what you are doing—it's nobody's business!"

"Okay, I will try. How are the boys?"

"They are okay, but they do not know about the move yet. I can't tell them because Tyrone will find out. I have to go to work. Tell your grandma I said hello." *Click.*

23
UP IN THE AIR

I went outside with Sissy, thinking to *myself, I don't know how Mom expects me to get us a place to stay. She had her whole extended family here, not to mention Dad's family as well. Can't she ask one of them to help find us a place to live?*

Just then, Frank pulled up with Walter and the girls. I was still pretty upset with Frank. I didn't want to see him, let alone talk to him. I decided to make my way down to the woods. I stayed down there until it got dark at which time I returned to Grandma's through the basement, up the stairs, and through the kitchen. I saw my cousins visiting with my grandparents. I didn't see Frank, but I heard him call me into the living room. I pretended not to hear him, and I made my way up into the attic and went to bed.

The next morning, I joined my grandparents for a very nice breakfast. After we ate and cleaned up, I asked Grandpa if I could have the classified section of the newspaper, which he gave me with no questions asked. My grandparents didn't know what was going on, but in due time they would. I made my way back up to the attic where I proceeded to look through the classified section for apartments throughout the day. There were so many places for rent: the east, west, north, and south sides. There were furnished apartments and unfurnished apartments. I didn't even know what furnished means. I spent the entire day looking for a place to live.

As I continued to look, I noticed the unfurnished apartments were much cheaper. I circled the places I thought fit our needs. It was too late to call about these places tonight. I will work on it first thing in the morning.

The next morning, I joined my grandparents and Walter for breakfast. Grandma had made her famous toast parties once again. I would never get tired of having breakfast with them. Once done we all retired to the living room to visit. Grandma began to ask all the same questions about things back in Rockford. In the past, I would tell her certain things, but now, I was here to stay, and I didn't want to talk about it. She was real slick about getting stuff out of me, like making me cookies or cake. She knew something was going on. She was kept out of the loop, and she didn't like it.

"Joey, I unpacked all of your bags. Why did you bring so much stuff?' "Because I always run out of clothes, Grandma. I always forget to pack some of my favorite clothes. This way, it is better to have too many than not enough, right?"

"You know I always have clothes for you here."

"You do if I want to dress like a nerd."

"Is there another reason why you packed so much, Joey?" *Please get off my back* was running through my mind. I took Sissy and went to the woods. I loved it down there. I didn't have to deal with people. My grandparents were great people, and I had never misled them, but this time was different. This was the only chance to get away from Tyrone. I could never live with myself if I was the one who slipped up and opened my big mouth about the move up here. If I told her why all the clothes were here, I was afraid she may say something to somebody, which in turn would get back to him.

After spending all day in the woods, I sulked back through the front door. There was Grandma and Grandpa in the living room watching *Hee Haw*. I didn't think Grandpa even noticed me come into the house. Not Grandma—she didn't miss a beat.

"Joey, where have you been, honey?"

"I was in the woods, walking on the Indian trails."

"Okay, honey," she said with a smile.

"Get ready for bed, please." I had a routine at bedtime that had not been changed for years. I would first take a bath, read for a while, and then call it a night. She would come up to the attic to tuck me in every night. Tonight was no different. Even though she knew I was upset before, she never brought it up. I thought for sure she would dig for information but not tonight. After I got into bed, she kneeled and led me through a few prayers. That was our routine. I kind of liked it. I never had structure at home, so this was different in a good way.

Early in the morning, I awoke to the sweet smell of coffee. Mom drank coffee, too, but the smell of Grandma's coffee had a soothing effect on me.

When I would wake up to the smell of Mom's coffee, I knew it was going to be a long, stressful day. I ate a quick breakfast. I then grabbed the paper and made my way back up to the attic. Once I got dressed, I studied the classified section of the newspaper. I was looking hard for apartments for rent. There were so many different options; I really didn't know exactly what we could afford or what Mom really wanted.

I made my way back downstairs into the kitchen. The phone started to ring. Grandpa climbed out of his chair to answer it, "Hi June, how are you" he responded. I stood by him so I could hear my mother's response.

"I'm doing good here. I'm just preparing to move up there."

"Oh, that's great news! Joey is right here, take care."

"Hi, Mom, how are you?"

"Busy, so what's up, have you found anything yet?"

"There are several places, Mom, but I'm not sure if we need a furnished or unfurnished apartment."

"We need a furnished apartment, Joey, I don't have a stove or refrigerator to bring up there. I need you to get busy today and make some phone calls! I have sent you $150, which should be enough for a deposit. Most landlords expect that. Make sure you don't spend the money on anything else—understand?"

"I've been looking, so cut me some slack!"

"Just remember, do not give anyone this phone number, Tyrone can't find out what I'm up to. Bye." She hung up quickly. I handed the phone back to Grandpa. He winked at me, and now I had a better idea what to search for. With any luck, we will have a place to live in no time.

I became so involved in what I was doing at the kitchen table that I didn't notice when Grandma returned home from the bread store.

"What are you doing, honey?" she asked with a puzzled look on her face.

"Grandma, my mom is moving all of us kids to Dubuque. She told me to start checking the newspaper for a place to live. I need to make some calls right now."

"Honey, no one is going to believe you. You are just a little kid; the landlord will think it is a practical joke."

"I have to try. If I am honest and tell them what is going on, I think someone will listen. Also, Mom has sent money here that I will use to secure the right place."

"How are you going to go around town to look at the places, Joey?" Grandpa asked.

"I don't know. I guess I will cross that bridge when I get to it." I know this; I will do anything and everything to make this happen! If Dad or Mom were here, this all would be easier. This move could mean that we would be reunited after all this time." I dreamed about that day for so long.

I made three calls in a matter of five minutes, and every one of those potential landlords blew me off.

"I don't rent to people that have small children." *I am not going to stop. I am going to keep going until I can't do this anymore.* I began to think maybe Grandma was right after all.

Mom put me up to this; it was not the first time she's done things like this to me. I quickly discovered this was harder than I thought, and as a result I became a little discouraged after a day of making these phone calls. Grandpa must have noticed this.

"Joey, don't worry. If it is meant for you to be the one who is to find a place, I promise that will happen. You need to put the newspaper away and get to bed." I didn't realize how late it was. I do need to get to bed, so I can do this all over again tomorrow. In the Saturday paper, I found an apartment that was close to what Mom was looking for. It had three bedrooms, furnished, on the bus line, and close to the schools. I was excited about the possibilities. I was a little gun shy to make that call. After yesterday's experiences, I began to think about having to go back to the life in Rockford. I picked up that phone and dialed the first number with all the courage in the world.

The phone on the other end rang forever before a man finally answered it.

"Hello," he said.

"How can I help you?"

"Hi, I'm calling about the apartment for rent. I know it is odd that I am making this call, but my mom is in Rockford in the process of moving up here. She asked me to look for a place. The apartment you have is what we are looking for. Can I come by to look at it?"

"Sure," came from the other end of the phone.

" Do you know when you want to come by?"

"Well, I will have to get back to you about the time, and just to let you know I am serious. I will put the deposit down to secure it for us!"

"Okay, just give me a call back, kid." *Click* the phone went dead.

I was so happy this guy took me seriously. I couldn't wait to go see the place. Now it was time to ask someone about taking me to go and look at the apartment.

Grandpa asked me to let Sissy out to use the bathroom. I decided to take her to the woods. While down there, all kinds of thoughts ran through my mind. *I can't believe how close I was to be coming a resident in Dubuque.* When I went back to the house, Grandma arrived. I waited for her to get out of her car, so that I could tell her about the potential apartment.

"Hi Gram, how are you doing?"

"Good, Joey, can you help me with the groceries please?"

"Sure, let me put Sissy in the house, and I will help." As we unloaded the car, we didn't say much to each other. After we put all the groceries in the kitchen, I told her I had some good news.

"Gram, I think I found an apartment for my family. I am so happy."

"Do you really believe this landlord took you seriously, Joey? I am sure he has some doubts, right?"

"Well I told him the whole story, everything, and he seemed to understand. Besides, once he sees I have the deposit, I am sure he would be fine with everything."

"So how are you going to go look at the place?"

"I was hoping you would take me...please."

"Your Grandpa is a landlord; he built this house in fact, so he knows if an apartment is up to snuff."

"Okay, can you ask him for me?"

"No, you need to ask him, I am sure he would be glad to help you." Well, I knew he was in Walter's bedroom watching TV, so now was not a good time, but as soon as he comes out, I will ask him. We had a great relationship. It was more of a father-son relationship. I knew this was Dad's place really, but he is not around.

The day seemed to drag by. Grandpa finally emerged from Walter's room, Thank God! At the dinner table, I asked Grandpa the big question.

"Grandpa, can you take me to look at the apartment that I called about today?"

"Sure, Joey, set up a time, and we will meet the landlord." *Wow, that was so easy.* I was holding my breath waiting for his answer. I was prepared to be let down as was my life to this point, but maybe he saw what was really happening and was all for it. With that, I looked at Grandma with a tear in my eye. She had the biggest smile on her face. This was coming together after all.

After dinner, I called the landlord and arranged to meet with him tomorrow morning. He was so nice about everything. Okay, now I wanted to call Ma to give her an update. Grandma had her phone in the corner of the living room, near the kitchen. When I called Ma to tell her the good news, she answered the phone drunk as a skunk! That brought me back down to earth fast. *What was she doing?* She was going to blow it. She had a habit of getting drunk and running her mouth. I didn't think she would say anything to him, but if she leaked the move to one of his sisters or brothers, the result would be the same. I would be forced back there because he will stop the move.

"Ma, I think I found a place for us to live."

"That's good, Joey. Just get the place set up. Is your Dad around? We will need his help."

"No, Ma, he is not here! Why are you drinking? Now, I am worried about you."

"Don't worry about me! I am fine. I am your mother; I don't have to answer to you about why I am drinking. I have a lot of stress in my life right now. Okay?" *Click.* She hung up on me. She hung up on me! I cannot believe it. What did I do now?

It was 8 a.m. when Grandpa came up to the attic.

"Time to get up, kid; the day is wasting away. Let's get breakfast done, so we can look at the apartment." Grandpa never came up to the attic to check on me or at least that I could remember him ever doing so.

"Okay, Grandpa." With that, I got dressed, made a beeline to the kitchen, and ate a couple powdered donuts while Grandpa drank his coffee.

"Joey, call the landlord and let him know we are heading down to look at the apartment."

"I will," I said.

"Hey, Grandpa, do you have the money I gave you?"

"Yep, I have it."

"Great."

I called Mike the landlord to let him know we were on the way down. Grandpa finished his coffee and away we went. As it turned out, the apartment was only a few blocks away from my Aunt Grace's house. Awesome. Once we got there, Grandpa did most of the talking. I mean Grandpa did not waste any time getting to business. I overheard Grandpa ask Mike to show him the apartment. I followed the two of them up a flight of stairs. It was a nice-looking place. I was ready to give my right arm for the place. I followed Grandpa as the landlord led us around the apartment. It had three bedrooms, a small kitchen, and a big living room. I really liked it. Even though it was a second-floor apartment with no air conditioning, I realized beggars can't be choosy. I was running out of time. Ma will be here in just few days. If for some reason, I didn't secure this place, I would really be in trouble. I got bored with the whole exercise and decided to go back outside. It was there

I had a chance to take in the area around the apartment. It was on Central, a busy street. I walked around to where the back yard was and couldn't believe how nice it was. It was a decent-sized yard. I walked out to the front at which time I noticed the school just a block up the street. I was so hoping Grandpa found the place in good enough shape for us to live.

Grandpa and Mike exited the building. Grandpa walked in my direction.

"Joey, come here. I want to talk to you," he said." I sure hope he thought it was a good deal. I had my fingers crossed.

"So…is it okay, Grandpa? Can we move in?"

"I don't see any issues with this place. I think you guys could be happy here. Are you sure your Ma wants an apartment on such a busy street?"

"She doesn't care about that. She just wants a place that's big enough and not run down."

"Well…" He paused as he looked at the ground as Mike stood behind him looking on.

"It looks like you have a new address." A huge smile crossed his face. I was so happy.

"Thank you, Grandpa." I said as I gave him a huge hug..

With money in hand, I made my way over to Mike's truck. I could see him working on some paperwork. Grandpa walked behind me and informed him of our intentions.

"Wonderful," he said, "I will need $150, please."

"Here you go, sir." I said.

"He will need a receipt to prove he paid the deposit, Mike," Grandpa said.

"No trouble, I will need you to fill out this rental agreement for me, please"

"I am not filling that out! I am not living here."

"Okay, Joey, your mom will have to fill it out when she gets here," Mike stated as a matter of fact. He returned his attention to some form on his clipboard. He then looked at me and said, "I usually don't allow this, but under these circumstances, we will get this done."

"Thank you, thank you very much, sir." I gave him a firm hand-shake. I was so happy. I had a place for us to live. I wanted to call Ma and let her know. I knew it would be a huge relief for her.

As Grandpa drove back to his house, he said, "Walter and I will help you guys move in, honey. In fact, I have a set of bunk beds you can have."

"Thanks, Grandpa." I was so excited. Once we got home, we were greeted by Grace and her girls, who were in the living room visiting Grandma. I thought Grandpa was more excited than me. He didn't wait to share with everyone the good news.

"That is awesome, Joey." Grace said.

"I will help you guys move in." I felt so loved and thrilled all at the same time. Things were looking up!

Just like clockwork, Mom showed up on Tuesday morning with the few belongings we had. Walter, Grandpa, and I had already been at the apartment, hauling up the beds. I was happy to see my family. But now was not the time to visit. The boys got to work along with Toots and Mom. My cousins Donna and Jane were here as well. They brought needed household items. In a matter of hours, we had everything in the apartment and set up. The only people who were "No Shows" were Dad and Grace—no big deal. None of Grace's girls were here, either, which caused me to be disappointed. Grandpa and Walter came into the living room to say goodbye. We were taking a break from all the work. The apartment was so hot. All of us kids were huddled around the two box fans we had.

"Hey, June. We are going to head out," Grandpa said. "You all are welcome to come up Sunday for dinner. I can ask Grace to pick you up."

"I will see," Mom responded. With that, they left. I was hoping we could go. I so loved spending time up there.

24
A BROKEN DREAM

I n a flash, Sunday was here. I reminded Mom that we were invited to Grandma's for dinner.

"You can go to your Grandma's, but I'm taking the kids over to Donna's. You need to find a way up there."

"Okay, I will call Grace to see if she can pick up pick me up."

I called Grace in the morning, and she agreed to pick me up. We were playing in the backyard when Grace pulled up in the driveway. I said my goodbyes to the boys, and climbed into Grace's car. I was still mad at her for not helping us move in. It meant a lot to me that she would have helped

As I jumped in the back seat next to those girls, they all said hi .I responded "Hi, guys." Once we got to Grandma's I followed the girls into Grandma's house. Grandma and Grandpa were in the living room, sitting in their normal spots: Grandma on her couch and Grandpa on his recliner. They were visiting with a man I never met before.

"Hi Joey. This is your uncle Jeff, your dad's younger brother." I walked over to where Jeff was sitting to shake his hand. As he stood up, I noticed his hands look kind of weird, like there was no muscle tone. They looked very weak.

"Hi, Joey, nice to finally meet you. I've heard some very good things about you."

"Thank you, Jeff. I appreciate that. It's nice to meet you as well. Do you live in Dubuque?"

"Yes, I recently moved here from Cedar Rapids." He was a good-looking man. He looked like Dad to me. He was tall with a medium build. He had brown hair and brown eyes.

We spent the next half hour or so just visiting with my grandparents, Grace, and her girls, but I was still really upset with Grace, and I guess she sensed that. After dinner Grace asked me to come outside with her. I followed her out the front door and sat down next to her on the front stoop.

"Joey, I can tell you're upset with me. I'm sorry I did not help you move into the apartment. I know how very important that was." I couldn't even look at her in the face up until now. Once I heard those words, the floodgates opened up. She put her arms around me.

"Grace, you said you were going to help us move. This has been a huge moment in all our lives. You are very important to me and my brothers. I'm just really hurt that you didn't show up."

"I understand that, Joey. Please understand this. I'm still upset with your mother, and I have not been able to forgive her for backing out of the adoption! It hurt me to the core. I love you very much, and although the adoption did not take place, I still consider you my son." We both stood up and hugged each other.

"I love you, Grace, and I'm so glad to finally be in Dubuque. Do you think you can get in touch with my dad?"

"I have been making phone calls. I'm working on that. I'll do my very best, I promise.

"Let's go back inside to visit with the rest of the family." I followed her back to the house, feverishly wiping the tears from my cheeks and regaining my composure before I went back around everybody else.

Jeff was in the kitchen at the sink. He called me over to him. I walked to where he was standing. He seemed like he wanted to ask me something.

"Joey, I really could use some help with cleaning my apartment. I'm handicapped. The everyday chores are very difficult for me. I was wondering if you and your brothers could help me with that maybe once a week or every other week. What do you think? I will certainly pay you guys. I can't pay you a lot because I'm on a fixed income, but I'll take care of you boys. Don't worry."

"I definitely would be willing to help you, Jeff, and I'm sure my brothers would, too."

"Okay, it's a plan then. I'll get your phone number from you later, and we'll set up a time when we can all meet."

"Okay, sounds good."

A short time later we all said our goodbyes before Grace, the girls, and I leave.

When I got back to the apartment, it was dark outside and from the street I could see all the lights were off in the apartment. Where could they be? They couldn't be in bed yet. I walked up the stairs. The door was locked. I pounded on the door—no answer. Being locked out of the apartment, not knowing where anyone was caused me to become very frustrated! We didn't have a car, so they couldn't be too far, could they? I decided to go through our backyard behind the apartment building toward Broadway. I took a shortcut, and sure enough, it took me very close to where Donna lived. She was my cousin. Donna had made several trips to Rockford over the past several years with her mom Dorothy.

Likewise, we spent a good amount of time at Donna's place. When I realized where the apartment was in town, I was instantly excited. I mean what were the chances we would move to a place that was so close to everything, including my wonderful extended family. As I approached the front door, I could hear my sister's voice. I rapped on the door a few times before Toots let me in. We made small talk as we walked into the kitchen. Mom was sitting at the kitchen table with Donna and Karen smoking a cigarette. She seemed as happy as a lark. The fact that we were here in Dubuque had begun to sink in. The only thing missing was Leon and Andre! After all the small talk, I finally had a chance to ask Mom where my brothers were. Up until now, I was under the impression that the boys were coming later. I guess you can call it wishful thinking. Mom was lucky to get herself here in one piece as it turned out. Toots motioned me into the living room; she wanted to talk to me. Before I could walk out to the living room, Mom said.

"The boys are not moving here. I could not pull it off, so don't ask me about it again, you creep!" I really didn't know what to say in response to the latest twists of my family saga. I walked out into the living room to where Toots was sitting. We hugged each other through our tears. I was crushed with this latest twist!

With summer ending, Mom's drinking had become very heavy once again. She was a heavy drinker before, but this was ridiculous. By getting away from Tyrone, I thought the drinking would stop, but not so much! It never failed every time she got drunk, she would sit me down in the kitchen at the table and lecture me on how everything was my fault. I would just sit there and go numb. A little bit of life would drain out of my body. She would force me to sit within an arm's length. The cigarette smoke was overwhelming. She would inhale her cancer sticks and slam beer after beer, crying her eyes out. On one night, she sat me down and started in on me.

"It's your entire fault, you little piece of crap. You are the reason Leon and Andre are not here!" I tuned her out and listened to the music playing in the background—"Papa was a rolling stone." I could see her mouth moving, but I couldn't hear anything coming out of it. I watched her slam another beer. She stumbled to the fridge for yet another. I saw my chance to escape to my room. Hopefully, she would let me sleep.

I laid in my bed for a few minutes. I knew she would come in and drag me back out to the kitchen at any moment. Instead, she found a new victim. Over the music, I could hear Toots screaming, "Mom, what's wrong with you? Stop grabbing me!" I jumped out of bed. She had been there to rescue me countless times; I was going to stop this.

When I entered the kitchen, there was Toots in the doorway of the bathroom trying to break free from Mom's grip. Mom kept hollering over the music, "You little tramp. Who do you think you are?" I stepped in and grabbed Mom by the waist with real determination. With one motion, I grabbed her and pulled her off Toots onto the floor.

"Leave her alone!" I hollered.

"Please go to bed!"

I turned away from Mom to check on Toots.

"Are you okay, man?" She was rubbing her arm, which was scratched and bleeding.

"I am okay. I'm going back to bed." Before I could react, Ma grabbed me from behind. Swinging wildly, she hit me right on the nose. I was a little dazed by her haymaker. I put her in a bear hug until she settled down. Suddenly Marty and Greg came running into the kitchen. With their help, we carried her to bed where she fell asleep. We didn't say one word. I could see in their eyes the hurt and the pain and how it was affecting them. Greg particularly seemed really bothered by it all. That's what made me and Greg different, I believed. Marty didn't receive the same type of terrible treatment from Mom that Greg and I did daily, and it affected us in a profound way. I went back to my room and fell fast asleep.

25
DOG DAYS

The school year had begun. Jefferson Middle School was several blocks east of the apartment. Since we didn't live more than a mile away, I didn't have the good fortune of riding the school bus, so I walked to school. The majority of the route was uphill. Both Marty and Greg were enrolled at Fulton, which was right across the street. Toots was enrolled at Hempstead High School. She caught the bus a block away. The walk gave me a chance to think about things. The first week was hard on me. I was still trying to come to grips with my youngest brothers not being here. From the very first day, I was given homework. Not only did I not understand the material, I didn't care to. My mind was on the welfare of my brothers. None of us kids talked to each other about how we felt about being away from the two boys. However, I could see how it was affecting all of them in different ways. When I was not at school, I tried to find things to do around the house Combined with the fact that Dad was nowhere around, I was daily fighting off the feelings of finally being away from Tyrone yet without my brothers. Jeff called my mom and set up a day and time to pick us up. He wanted to discuss working for him.

Jeff picked us up Saturday afternoon and took us to Hardee's restaurant. Hardee's restaurant was a fast-food joint, but it was unlike any other place we've ever been to. Sure, we have been to McDonald's, Gerry's and Burger King on very rare occasions, but this was a special treat. As we entered the restaurant, Jeff said we could order whatever we wanted. This was so uncommon. And of course, my brothers took full advantage. They ordered so much food I didn't know where they're going to put it all.

I didn't want to take advantage of Jeff's generosity, so I just ordered a cheeseburger, fries, and a drink. I was content with that. We found a booth to sit in. After we made quick work of our meals, Jeff proceeded to tell us what he could use our help with.

"So, boys I don't know if Joey had told you that I am physically handicapped, I have Charcot-Marie-Tooth disease. Which means I have trouble using my hands and feet. Eventually I may end up in a wheelchair. There are a lot of things I can no longer do. In fact, I don't work. I am on a fixed income. I really can use some help around my place with cleaning, mopping, dusting, and vacuuming. If you guys want to help me, I can put you to work right away. Greg spoke up.

"When can we start? Can we start now?"

"No, Joey, let's shoot for next Saturday. I'll pick you guys up at let's say 1 p.m. How does that sound?"

"It sounds good to me. What do you guys think, Greg and Marty?"

"Sure, man," Marty responded.

"Yes" was Greg's response.

"Okay then, boys, it sounds like a plan. I'll set it up with your mother, and if you guys do a good job, I will see no reason why we can't do this long-term. In fact, I would like to do things with you guys and maybe catch a hockey game or go to concerts and things like that." I began to cry a little bit. The fact that Jeff, who I've never met before, wanted to not only help us to make money but he wanted to invest in us is something a dad should be doing. None of us had that, and I think we are all really excited about what the future held. True to his word, Jeff picked us up that first time to clean his apartment, and that was the start of a wonderful relationship.

We've only been in Dubuque for about two months when Mom shared some good news with us after school on a Friday. Mom called all of us into the kitchen for dinner. As I entered I saw she was cooking up a big pot of macaroni and cheese—one of my favorite meals.

She was in a good mood for a change, so I knew there must be something in the air. Was Dad in town? Did she get a job?

"Hey kids, I have some wonderful news. I had applied for us to live in Sheridan Village, the new housing project is on the north end of town. We've been accepted."

Toots, Marty, and Greg jumped up from the table and gave Mom a huge hug. I sat there with many thoughts running through my mind. *What will change? Just our physical address? Will she go back to the way she once was, sober and loving. I missed my mother.*

"When are we are moving, Mom?" Toots asked.

"Well I signed a lease with this landlord for six months. I've spoken with him about getting out of the lease, but he has not responded to my request yet. The worst-case scenario would be we lose the deposit. The manager at the new place wants us to move in next week. I explained to him my situation with the release. He responded by saying that's not his problem. If we don't move in a reasonable amount of time, they will rent the apartment to somebody else. I need you guys to start packing up your clothes. I have boxes from Eagle supermarket. Toots, I need you and Joey to help Marty and Greg to ensure they get all the stuff packed nice and neat." I contained my excitement because Dad still was not here, not to mention Leon and Andre were still in Rockford. To be honest, I was hoping her good news was the fact that the boys would be moving here.

Later that evening, the landlord came to the apartment. He sat at the kitchen table explaining to Mom that she was bound to the contract she signed. All of us kids sat as she proceeded to share with him our plight. Not having her youngest kids here must have pulled on his heartstrings. He allowed Mom to get out of the lease. And just like that, we moved into the new apartment. We had the second apartment on the left. It was very nice. Everything was brand new. It was so much better than the dilapidated apartment we had been living in. Maybe this change was what I need to get through the school year.

Jeff had been utilizing us boys on a weekly basis. That was one of the few bright spots in my life. Since we moved, Dad had not been around. For all I knew, Mom didn't tell him where we moved. I didn't want to be around him if he was drunk. I mean as much as I wanted him in my life, I never thought it would turn out like it had.

Same Old Crap

With the end of the first quarter, school was still not going very well. I was failing the 8th grade! I didn't need a report card to tell me that, I thought I'd make new friends, but that didn't pan out as planned, either.

In the classroom, some of the students and teachers were treating me differently than the other kids. I didn't really fit in or belong. It could be in part because of our family, not having a dad around and certainly about my brothers in Rockford. Kids in the neighborhood learned about our condition, so word got around that my family was in distress and not your normal family. What I mean is having a black stepdad and two younger brothers that are mixed is not the norm in Dubuque. They put a label on us, and as a result, we were all treated as inferiors.

My sister and brothers didn't seem like they were struggling in school like I was. Mom's drinking intensified when she couldn't find steady work. We were really struggling to survive. She was receiving welfare. Along with the welfare, we got the free government cheese and powdered milk. We got these items on a regular basis. I didn't like the cheese, and I could never mix the powdered milk right. I would just drink water like it was going out of style.

On many days, all we had to eat were sugar sandwiches. I would take a piece of bread, spread a little butter on it, and cover it with sugar. This was a breakfast of champions. I really blamed mom. She wasn't trying hard. She was away from home, and she wasn't staying sober. Now that Tyrone was out of the picture, I thought Ma would go back to the way she used to be. She was so loving and caring before Tyrone, but now she was treating me worse than before. I didn't understand it at all.

On Friday, I rode my dirt bike down to school like any other day. We couldn't afford a nice heavy-duty chain to lock my bike up. What I had was a combination lock with a little thin-gauged metal chain. It wasn't much to brag about.

My bike was black and red with heavy-duty rims and forks. A lot of kids in my new neighborhood and many kids at school liked the bike. Random kids complimented me on the bike. I guess that was their way of letting me in. Little did I know that somebody would set me up that Friday afternoon. After school, I made a bee-line to the bike rack. It was then I discovered my bike was gone. I thought my eyes were playing tricks on me. I looked on the ground. There it was—my theft-proof, top-of-the-line chain cut in half. I was crushed. I went back into the school to the principal's office to explain what happened. They assisted me by calling the cops. Once the police show up, I filled out a report with the description of the bike and some other paperwork. They tried to assure me that the bike would reappear. I wished I could believe that. Oh, to come to school on Monday and find my bike back in the rack. Yeah, that was dreaming! Once I finished up, they sent me on. I could hold back the tears during that process, but once I began the long walk home, it all came out.

When I got back to the projects, I walked down to talk to Kevin, one of my new friends in the neighborhood. I asked him to please keep his eyes out for my bike.

"I will keep my eyes peeled. That was really messed up—what happened to you. I have a skateboard you can use if you need it."

"Thanks, Kevin, I have a skateboard, too, but thank you for the offer." Later that night, I built up the courage to tell Mom. She was indifferent to my plight, even though she knew my love for that bike.

"What do you want me to do? Pull a new one out of my butt?" I couldn't believe she just said that. How could she be so cruel after all this time away from the monster? I knew we couldn't afford a new bike.

"I'm not asking for a bike. I have my skateboard. I will make do. I always have.

The following Monday after school, I was greeted by my aunt Lynn. She was in the kitchen with Ma. There was a dense fog of cigarette smoke in the kitchen as I entered.

"Hey, Joey, how you are doing?"

"I'm okay. I have a lot of homework. Mom didn't even acknowledge me. She usually didn't unless she was ticked off or just wanted someone to hit on.

"Joey, I have something for you outside," Lynn said with a big grin on her face. Her eyes were bloodshot from all the smoke. She was really excited about this gift. I mean I had never seen her so excited. Not to mention the fact that she practically ran outside of the front door ahead of me. What could she possibly have for me outside? She was poor, just like us.

I made it outside and there around the corner was a big, green old-man bike, fenders included.

"Your sister told me you needed a bike. I was at St. Vincent's, and I saw this one. I thought of you, so I bought it. Do you like it?"

"Thanks a lot, Lynn. It looks too big for me, though."

"I didn't want to hurt her feelings, but it looked like a green truck, a big, heavy, old-fashioned bike that belonged to some old dude. It was then that I realized just what this bike meant to me. My aunt showed her love. The look of the bike was not that important. What was important was where the bike came from, and who gave it to me.

I went for a long bike ride. When I returned I saw Greg and Marty running into the apartment. I thought maybe someone was chasing them. When I arrived, both boys were frantically explaining what had just happened.

"We were lighting firecrackers across the street in the big apartment complex and we were seen by the managers wife!" Greg exclaimed.

"You dumbasses! Why did you do that?" Mom hollered back.

"Sorry Ma!" Marty blurted.

She jumped up from her lair at the kitchen table and began to swing wildly at Greg.

"Mom stop!" I demanded as I stormed into the kitchen and positioned myself between her and Greg.

"They made a mistake! Beating them does nothing to fix it." I shouted trying to make her stop swinging at Greg.

She quickly turned her wrath toward me. "Who do you think you are cocksucker?" She screamed with her index finger an inch from my face. "Mind you own business! And another thing…"

Before she could continue there was a knock on the door. It was not a friendly knock but one with bad intent.

"I will deal with you in a minute moron." She staggered out of the kitchen and to the front door.

We were curious of who it would be. As she opened the door we saw the property manager and hs wife. "Hey June I have been informed that your boys were lighting firecrackers in one of our buildings. No one was hurt, thank God! However this is a serious offense." As he continued to rattle on about the rental agreement do's and don'ts Marty and Greg must have thought this was a good time to go to bed. I refocused my attention back on Mom. "We also have had several reports of you walking around the area harassing folks. In fact, in the reports I have received people complain that you appeared drunk. I have added this complaint to your file as well. If this behavior continues I will be forced to serve you an eviction notice." He handed her his report and he and his wife left.

Mom said nothing. She returned to the kitchen, opened the fridge and grabbed another beer. I knew it was definitely time for me to go to bed.

We were all worried that our stay here would be short lived and an eviction notice would be coming soon. Truth be told if we are evicted it has more to do with Mom and her drinking. On more than one occasion just like the property manager said, Ma would get drunk and terrorize the neighbors. These behaviors continued and Steve the property manager had to call the house several times. He informed us that Mom was at a neighbor's apartment, arguing with the residents. As it usually would go, some of the other drunks would invite Mom over to drink a few beers. She would get drunk and act a total fool. I guess Ma is lucky we were there to bail her out. The other option is she could have been arrested.

26
MONSTER MASH

only had two friends. Kevin was a tall, lanky kid, who loved to play basketball. David was a few years younger than me. He was handicapped; he had an artificial leg. Apparently, when he was a toddler, his dad ran over him with a lawnmower.

When the three of us played basketball, David tried his very best. I always tried to encourage him. There was a boy that lived near us named Bruce. He typically came down to play basketball with us. He was such a bully. He always picked on David, calling him a crippled handicap. I got fed up one day.

"You need to shut up and leave him alone. He's my friend!" David didn't have any brothers, and his father drove the city bus, so he was never around. I made it my duty to protect him from kids like Bruce.

He responded.

"Hey pussy! I'm going to kick your butt after this game!" I ignored him. I have heard it all before. I could defend myself. I was not worried about him.

Sure enough, as soon as the game (which we won) was over, Bruce attacked me from behind. We were about the same size. However, I had the upper hand because I had been in some bad battles. I proceeded to beat him soundly. I looked on as he walked away licking his wounds like a cur dog. I walked David back to his apartment. I wanted to ensure there were no more surprises coming from the bully.

Spring Break

I had been away from my two youngest brothers for six months now. I really missed them. Once or twice a week, Mom would call Rockford to talk to them. We all took our turn to talk to them. It was so nice. It also made it that much harder for me. Tyrone usually wanted to talk to all of us, but I refused to talk to him. I had nothing to talk to that monster about. After we talked to the boys, I heard Mom tell Tyrone, "We are being evicted. Marty and Greg got caught setting fireworks off in the neighbors hallway and set the woods on fire!"Even though I knew we were getting evicted hearing Mom tell Tyrone really upset me. Mom saw me listening and screamed " Go get lost, you creep!"

I ran outside to track down Toots. I found her at the basketball court hanging out.

"Toots, can I talk to you, man?"

"What is it?"

"I need to talk to you in private." As she walked over to me, I began to cry.

"What's wrong, dude?"

"We are being evicted."

"Yeah, right!"

"I am being serious. Remember when the boys got caught with the firecrackers and set the woods on fire and the fire department was called to put it out?"

"Yes, I remember."

"Well because of that, according to Ma, they decided to kick us out."

"Let's go talk to Ma," she said. As we made our way back to the apartment I asked, "Where are we going to live, Toots? Mom's family always says they are there for us. It looks like this will be yet another opportunity for them to step up. I already know they will let us down—all of them. Mark my words!"

"Man, you worry too much! We already know Dad is not helping. I am used to being let down. All we can do is stay positive and pro-active," Toots remarked. She is so wise beyond her years. Instantly, I was calm. That was until we walk into the apartment.

Mom was sitting on the living room floor smoking a cancer stick and guzzling a beer. She was wailing into the phone.

"Mom," Toots said.

"We need to talk! Why didn't you tell us that we were getting evicted?" Mom abruptly hung up the phone and struggled to get on her feet.

"Because it is none of your business, heifer."

"Mom, drinking is not going to make this any better!" I said.

"I need another beer." She stumbled to the back of the room where she had stashed her booze. Toots and I walked back outside. We just stood there as we cried our eyes out. Finally, Toots spoke up.

"Joey, you need to be strong for the boys. I got a feeling we are going back to Rockford."

"I think the same thing." At least we'd all be together—but at what cost?

Sure enough, the next day Mom informed us that we were indeed moving back with Tyrone. Over the next several days we began the difficult task of packing our clothes and a few other items. I have been through this years ago. Nothing changed then and I doubt things will improve back under the same roof as Tyrone.

27
BUMP AND GRIND

I t was Saturday morning during Easter break. I awoke to a voice I was all too familiar with. I could hear Tyrone downstairs talking to Mom! All the sudden I heard two sets of feet running up the stairs. Leon was leading the way. He and Andre jumped onto my bed.

"I'm so happy to see you guys." We hugged each other for a long time. I could not get over how big they were getting. All of us kids were together again!

Moving Day

The St. Vincent truck showed up bright and early. St Vincent was a local thrift shop. They catered to the down-and-out population in town. We had shopped there many times. Over time I think everything Mom had purchased came from there. When a family had household goods to donate, Vinnie's would send a truck to pick up the items or deliver items as needed.

They loaded up the beds, dressers, and all the stuff that we had accumulated up to this point. Those beds came from my Grandpa. They had sentimental value to me, but we have nowhere to put them in Rockford. After Vinnie's left with the few items we gave them, it was time to finish packing our clothes.

After all the packing was done, we had a quick breakfast, and on the road back to Rockford. As we crossed the Mississippi River,

I once again caught the smell of the bakery It was my hope and desire to return someday. Maybe my dad will pull his act together.

The drive to Rockford usually took well over two hours but not with Tyrone driving! It was just over one and a half hours when we entered the city limits. He was driving like a man possessed. His first stop was Central Park Tap of all places. This neighborhood liquor store was his favorite place. All that he truly loved was behind those walls. We all were going to be made painfully aware of that fact. Tyrone finally emerged from the store carrying a big paper bag.

I leaned forward and whispered to Toots, "Bet you a penny it's booze and cigarettes, man."

"Dude, I am not betting you. I know what it is!" Once we got home, we started the big job of unloading the car. We didn't have the car unpacked yet and he was already drinking his prize. It was going to be the same old bump and grind.

I didn't know how Ma fell for his lies. I could tell he was the same cat just with a new game. We didn't have much with us, so before long, we all settled into our bedrooms downstairs. During our trip home, Leon and Andre filled us in with what was going on in their lives. There was so much they wanted to show us. It was great to be with those two again. I missed them so much. I never ever wanted to be apart again! Mom enrolled me at Wilson Junior High School. It was directly across from McIntosh School.

I had lost contact with many of my friends from my grade school days. Now at Wilson, I could reconnect. I was extremely happy about this fact.

I really focused on my schoolwork. I didn't know if the material was easier than in Dubuque, or if I was more focused. The last two and a half months of eighth grade were a breeze.

Things were better at home initially with Ma and Tyrone. At least that was what he wanted people to think. Toots and I knew he had not changed one bit. He was constantly going here or there while Ma would be at work on second shift. He would keep all of us boys in the basement, locked up tight, while he would take Toots with him, leaving me to fend for the boys by myself. In fact, there was a routine we boys had to follow after school each day.

When we arrived home from school we were instructed to grab a snack, such as cheese and crackers, and head to the basement. This was the routine day in and day out. Once all the other boys were downstairs, he locked the basement door, so we could not go upstairs. Even after we all finished our homework, we were detained in the basement until dinner. It really sucked.

My youngest brothers didn't understand this like I did. On one occasion, Tyrone informed me that he was heading to the grocery store. After he left the house with Toots, my brother Marty asked me a hypercritical question:

"Joey, what if there was a fire? How are we going to escape?"

I was at a loss for an answer.

"I don't know. Let's see if we can have one of you guys climb out through the basement window." The window was quite small, and as time went by I became more and more frantic as one by one my brothers could not fit thought the small space.

Just when I was about to give all hope for an escape route, my baby brother Andre said.

"I want to try." He was so young I didn't think he could do it. If he could, that would be our ticket out of there. So, Marty, Greg, and I helped him up to the opening of the window. He crawled right through. I told him once he got out to check the door to see if it was unlocked. I was hopeful he could enter the house and unlock the basement door to let us all out.

Well, as it turned out, he could not get into the house. Now what? Next thing I knew, Tyrone was home, carrying Andre in his arms.

"What the hell was he doing outside? I found him at Mables' house."

"We were afraid of being trapped down here. What if there was a fire?" I said.

"Tyrone looked at me and said, "There ain't going to be fire, boy!'" He then returned to his domain upstairs, locking the door behind him.

Later that night, Mom returned from work. When she opened the basement door the boys mobbed her. I tried to tell her about the latest, but Tyrone was within earshot.

"Your dumbass boy made Andre climb through the window. They were trying to get out of the basement. What is his problem?"

"You should not be locking them in the basement in the first place. There is something not quite right with you. That is the problem!"

After I heard this, I knew I was in trouble. I was the master-mind behind it all. I was the one who tried to upset the apple cart. I returned downstairs and got scarce because I knew what was coming. I didn't know if he got too drunk and forgot about the whole production or he was keeping a tally, but I didn't face his wrath for that incident the next day or even the next week. Heck, I must be scot-free! Maybe he had a change of heart.

It was not long before Mom started to sleep on the couch in the study. This was a glaring sign that things were not well. I mean he had gone back on his word and gotten drunk and beat her several times. I couldn't figure out why she never called the cops on him or leave again, this time with all the kids.

Lock Down

Tyrone had set up perimeters on the street we lived on.

"You can ride your bikes to both ends of the street and around the circle, but nowhere else. So, this was our summer of riding the bikes up and down the same street repeatedly. Except for the rare occasion when he would let me go to Sunset Park, I would never dare disobey except for one day.

I rode down Shelley Drive like I had a million times before, but this time was different. Once I got to Arthur, I just kept going, making a circle around the block. It felt so liberating, yet so scary. Part of me wanted to ride my bike even further, but the other part of me was afraid he would just appear out of nowhere and be really ticked off. After about an hour of riding this new route, I decided I had better get home. Normally, I was with Marty and Greg. We would ride together, but they were at home doing other things. It was good just to be able to relax and not have to look after those guys. We always made the best of this strange situation.

When I wheeled into the backyard, I could see Marty and Greg arguing with Leon. I didn't know what was going on, but everyone seemed upset.

"You are going away. Leon yelled at the boys.

"Leon, who is going away? What are you talking about? "I asked.

"Dad said he is going to take the three of you to a foster home. He doesn't want you anymore."

"What?" Marty said in disbelief.

"He is getting rid of you guys—you, Greg, and Joey." You could have heard a pin drop. Marty, Greg, and I all looked at each other in utter disbelief.

I could not believe my ears. First, what was going on, and why would my brothers tell us this? Did they want us to leave? Did they believe what their dad said about me? I was hurt. I put my bike away and went into the house.

I could not think straight. Toots was in the kitchen with Tyrone, playing cards. Usually I would jump in and play but not now. Here we go again; he wanted to get rid of us like garbage. I had been through this before. Last time, it was just me that was on the chopping block. Now it was the three of us.

28
I WILL FLY AWAY!

The summer flew by, and football practice was about to begin at Auburn. I really wanted to play. As long as I could remember, I enjoyed football. From a very young age, it was one of the things we boys did together. Tyrone would be the quarterback. We would get kids from our block to play against us. It was a lot of fun. The NFL was big in our house as well. Tyrone liked the Pittsburgh Steelers, and I liked anyone facing them. I was a huge Bears fan, but I liked the Cowboys, too. It would make my day when the Cowboys beat the Steelers. It was like a victory for me—the good guys, America's team as the Cowboys were called, against the Steelers, the bad guys.

The coaches sent me a letter to inform me of twice-a-day practices so we can get into "football shape." I knew I had my work cut out for me. I tried out for one of the corner back positions, but I just was not fast enough. I ended up on the offensive line at right guard.

After three weeks, the starting roster was revealed. I didn't get the right guard spot, nor did I get the middle linebacker position I had played on the defense. I was fortunate, as it turned out, to even make the team. I was one of the smallest kids on the team, and my lack of experience was pretty glaring to the coaches for sure. I ended up as the 3rd string, right guard. My job was to block the opposing player from getting to the quarterback. The quarterback's job was to either throw the football to a teammate or hand the ball off to a running back. To advance the football one hundred yards into the end zone was the goal. My position on the offensive line was one of five positions. We on the line were the backbone of the team

I was not really that disappointed. I mean, the main reason I joined was for the love of football, but also it was an excuse to stay away from the war zone at home. Things went back to the way they were before at home. I was looking for an out. I was hoping I would get some support from home when I played ball, but I didn't really expect it. The freshman team didn't have a big following. Most of the student body went to the varsity games on Friday nights. I didn't have any hopes of Mom coming to any of my games. After all, they were on Thursday afternoons, and she worked during that time.

During the second game of the season, as I sat on the bench, Tyrone showed up with Toots. I was so happy to see her, but not sure why he was here. He never supported anything I did. Sure enough, he began to point and laugh at me. David, who was sitting next to me, asked, "Who is that, Joey?"

"My stepdad," I said as I looked at the ground.

"What is his problem?" I could feel Tyrone staring at me. I always could. The hairs on the back of my neck stood up when I sensed that. Toots walked over by me and David and sat next to me.

"How you doing, man? Did you play yet?"

"No, I will play in the second half," I replied somewhat embarrassed.

"Well, he has to go see Gail. I just wanted to stop by to see my kid bro knock people around." She laughed.

"Okay, I will see you at home."

"Okay, cool dude." With that she walked away. I didn't even bother to look back at him. I just pretended to be into the game. My spirits were lifted by her visit. I loved her so much. We had been through so much together. Things were about to get worse for all of us again.

The first month of school was a blur. Things at home continued to deteriorate. They were both drinking a lot, and he was heavy-handed toward her. I really dreaded walking through the door every day after school because I never knew what to expect. The rumors of the three of us, Marty, Greg, and me, being given away never went away. It seemed like whenever Tyrone would be unhappy with something, he would matter of fact say, "You are just like your daddy, dumbass."

During this time, we were going to ride the Joy Bus to Church. On Sunday December 6th, 1981, the bus picked all us up at the house. Once there at the church, we made our way to our Sunday school classrooms. The classes were broken into different age groups. I was in one area, and the other boys were elsewhere. After Sunday school, there was a space of fifteen minutes before the church service would begin. I needed to go to the bathroom, so I made my way there. Greg was coming out of the bathroom as I was heading in.

"Joey, I need to talk to you, man." I didn't know what he wanted to talk about, but it seemed urgent based on the look on his face.

"Wait here," I said. He didn't. He followed me right into the bathroom. He looked around to make sure no one else was in the bathroom with us.

"We should run away. Tyrone has been threatening to send us to a foster home. Screw that, let's run away to Dubuque. You know they will take care of us there." Instantly, my heart began to beat fast as my adrenalin began to ramp up.

"How will we get to Dubuque, Greg? It's the dead of winter."

"Once we get out of town, we can just hitchhike. We will be fine—we will be careful."

"Okay, let's do it, we need to grab our coats, and sneak out the side door."

With the stealth of an alley cat, we got our items and went outside. I was so scared someone would catch us. If that happened, we would really get it.

We walked as fast as we could and took the quickest way to West State Street. West State was Highway 20 to Dubuque. As we made our way out of town, we both took a sigh of relief that we had made it this far. We continued walking along the highway, confident we could make it to Dubuque. I guess I didn't realize it at the time just how far it really was. We were about five miles out of town when a state trooper saw us on the highway. He was traveling in the other direction.

"Just keep walking, Greg, and don't look back. Maybe he will just keep going."

No such luck! I could hear the squeal of his car tires as he made a U-turn. He drove past us and pulled over. We kept walking straight ahead. *Does he know we are runaways? Did the church call and report us missing?* All these thoughts were running through my mind. Greg began to tear up a little bit.

"Let me do the talking," I told him. The officer approached us with a stern look on his face.

"What are you boys doing walking along the highway? Do you have a death wish?" I had to think fast. There was a farmhouse just up the road, and we had just passed several homes, so I had the perfect story.

"We are walking over to our friend's house, sir."

"Where is this friend's house?"

"You see the red house about two blocks away? That's it."

"Where did you come from? Where do you live?"

"I pointed at the white house we had passed a short time before. For all I knew, this could be his house, but I had to tell him something. I was determined to make it to Dubuque. This was just a small problem.

"Okay, boys, you need to get away from the road. Just be careful."

"Yes, sir," we both said. We began to walk again, watching him drive away. Once he was out of sight, we had to come up with a plan.

We immediately walked down into the cornfields on the right. We found a trail that was running east to west. It was perfect. We were down in a little valley, and we could not be seen from the highway, so we thought we had it made. We were so fired up and eager to get to Dubuque. In our hasty, last-second decision to run away, we never thought of taking any provisions such as water or food.

Thank God the weather was sunny and warm for a December day. We resorted to eating snow for the water. All I could think about was seeing Grandma's house with the front porch light on as if she knew we were on the way. After some time, the trail took us further north through a farmer's cornfield. Now by this time, it began to get dark. I knew it must be nearing 5 p.m. This was taking a lot longer than I thought. We didn't have any real landmarks to tell us where we were or how far we had walked, but we just stayed upbeat. After nightfall, we found ourselves still walking through these cornfields, but I had the sense we were not alone. It was a moonless night and it was very hard to see where we were.

"Just keep your eyes on the trail, Greg." We took turns leading the way. We came around a corner, and we saw cows everywhere.

"Joey, run!"

"Look! Don't run, just walk slow!" I was just as scared as he was. There were heifers and bulls within an arm's reach. That scared the crap out of both of us. I refused to let this stop us from our goal. We finally made it through, but the journey was about to get a lot more intriguing.

The temperature had dropped since sunset. We stopped a few times to rest. I knew Greg was worn out, but I had to encourage him.

"Come on, man, we have a long way to go."

On top of it all, it began to snow. What else could go wrong? Oh, God, please help us! We walked several more blocks then we saw in the distance a series of homes.

"Greg, do you see the houses over there? Maybe we can ask them for a ride to Dubuque. What do you think?"

"I think we should try."

"Okay, I will do the talking."

I saw a brick house on the end of the street. We decided to just tell whoever that answered we needed a ride to Dubuque. All they could say was no. What was the harm anyway? I lead the way onto the front porch. I could see through the window, there was a man in the house.

"Okay, Greg, come on, there is someone home." I rang the doorbell and held my breath as I watched the man approach the door.

"Hello, can I help you?"

"Well, Sir, my brother and I are trying to find a ride. It is very cold, and we are really tired."

"Where exactly are you boys heading?"

Before I could answer the man, Greg piped up, "We are going to Dubuque."

Oh no, I was going to tell him Freeport or Stockton. He isn't going to buy our story.

"Where are your parents?" He looked us over. I didn't know what to say.

"Excuse me for a minute." He made his way back into the house.

I looked at Greg with a look that could kill, "Let me do the talking from now on, Greg. You are going to screw this up." As I focused my attention back on the front door, I saw the man had put his coat on. That was when I noticed this guy was a state trooper. I leapt off the front porch as fast as I could.

"Run, Greg, he is a cop!" I flew up the road and jumped through a barbed wire fence into a cornfield. My adrenaline was pumping so fast, I lost track of Greg. I looked back and saw that he was hung up on the barbed wire fence. I ran back and freed him.

"Joey, you left me, you jerk!"

"I didn't leave you. I am here. Shut up; we need to get out of here." We began to run in what I thought was a westerly direction. I looked back in the direction of the house we had just ran from, and I saw people standing out in front of the property.

After I thought we were out of immediate danger, we both just collapsed from exhaustion. Cold, wet, thirsty, and hungry, Greg began to cry.

"Man. I don't want to do this anymore. We will never make it to Dubuque."

"I know we should have planned this better, but I hate so many things here. He hates us. So instead of him deciding where to send us, we sent him a message that he isn't in total control." I guess everything just hit both of us at the same time. The realization hit us that it was over.

We just sat there and cried for a while when we noticed the spotlights shining in the field we were hiding in. We could hear cars speeding by the country road with the sirens blaring.

"The trooper called in the cavalry, Greg. They will come in here after us."

"What do you want to do, Joey?"

"I saw the state police station up the street before. I say let's just walk over there and turn ourselves in."

"Let's do it," he said and with that, we made it to the highway.

As we were crossing the road, a state trooper came flying up to us.

"Hold it right there, boys." We stopped in our tracks.

"We are turning ourselves in, sir." Greg said. He didn't want them to think they found us. There was a difference, you know. Surprisingly, the cops were very nice to us. They took us into the headquarters and allowed us to watch *Sunday Night Football* while they called our folks. Then one of the officers came and took Greg to an officer by a big desk. He was out of earshot, but I could tell he was being asked a lot of questions. I was sure they thought I was the one to blame for all of this. Anytime now, the cops will question me as well. There was nothing I could do about it. I was truly happy to be warm, sipping on hot cocoa, and out of the crappy weather. I was so focused on the football game—Bears versus Buccaneers—I didn't notice Tyrone and Ma had arrived. Greg was excited to see them.

After all the niceties, we were loaded up in the car and heading home. It was the worse car ride of my life. No one said a word. I knew—I just knew—Tyrone was going to get me. That was a fact. So I was just preparing myself for it. Once we got home, Tyrone stopped me and Greg by the garage.

"Y'all stay here, you aren't going into my house with all that dirt on you." With that he went into the garage and pulled out a garden hose.

"June, go grab the camera from the study."

"Okay." When she came back, all my brothers and sister were with her.

"Everyone was looking for you, Joey. Where did you guys go?" Toots asked.

"They shut down the whole neighborhood looking for you, Joey," Ma finally piped up.

"Everyone from the church went looking. Why did you run away?"

"Because you guys don't want us. You hate us. Telling the boys you and Tyrone are taking us to a foster home. How am I supposed to feel?"

She just looked at me as if to say, "How dare you talk back to me!"

Without warning, Tyrone proceeded to spray us down with the garden hose, outside in the freezing weather no less. People treat pets better than this. All the while I could see Greg just crying nonstop. Not me, I was not about to let him enjoy this. I won't let it bother me.

"Once I get all the mud off you, you will strip and head right to the shower, understand?"

"Yes," we said. He was really taking his sweet time about this. Finally, when we thought he was done, he made us stand in place while he took pictures of us again. I guess a before-and-after picture, I don't know. It was very sick.

With the showers done, we were reunited with everyone downstairs. Marty had all these questions. He was all over the place, but I missed him a lot. Andre and Leon are young, but they are also a sight for sore eyes. I am just waiting for Tyrone to appear any moment to dish out the spanking. I knew he was planning something. Greg just kept crying because he was so afraid of what he will do next.

"Don't worry, Greg, just relax and do what he tells you. No need to make him more upset."

Before we knew it, 10 p.m. was here, and with that a holler from upstairs,

"Y'all go to bed" Tyrone bellowed. *He isn't going to tell me twice* I thought to myself.

"Did he forget, Joey?" Greg asked through the sobs.

"No, Greg, he didn't forget. He is probably planning something for later. Don't worry about it. Get some rest."

Monday morning was like every other dysfunctional day on Shelley Drive. We all got off to school. We usually walked unless it was as he said thirty below zero. If not, he demanded we walk, and I preferred to walk. I didn't need him away. Since football had finished, I joined the wrestling team. I really enjoyed it,

After school, I started to make my way to Wilson School for wrestling practice. Just as I walked past the football stadium, Tyrone pulled up.

"Get in the car." I climbed in the back seat right past Toots who was sitting up front. He drove over to McIntosh and moments later came out with Greg. I knew he had something in store for us, just not sure what. Before he made it to the car I asked Toots, "Where is he taking us, man?"

"I don't know. Ssshhhh!"

Greg climbed into the back seat as he and Tyrone joked and laughed about something. I didn't see what was so funny. In fact, this all seemed very serious to me. He would not even look at me the whole time as we traveled downtown.

"Where are we going, Dad? Greg asked.

"You will see, Greg, just hang on." He pulled in front of the Public Safety building.

"Toots, stay here; I will be right back."

"Okay." He led us up two flights of stairs into an interior of some strange building. Once they opened the door, I knew we were in jail. I turned to see where Greg was when I noticed Tyrone walked out of the room. Greg was there with a shocked look on his face.

"I told you, Greg. He was planning this. He is trying to scare us. Don't let his games faze you; stay strong."

"I will, "

Jail Birds

A rough-looking jailer came into the room. He was a lot bigger and taller than Tyrone. The look on his face said it all. I had seen that look before—every day in fact. In the presence of Tyrone, I saw it—a look of pure hate.

"So, you boys think it is cool to run away from home? This is where runaways always end up. Follow me."

The next thing I knew, we were separated. I was put in a dark cell all by myself. It was a very small cell. There was a toilet in the corner and a bed along the wall. The bed had no bedding on it, and the mattress was full of urine stains. The smell of urine was so strong that my eyes watered. One whole wall was filled with graffiti. I saw a lot of gang symbols. I recognized many of the code names on the wall of shame. This was just a calling card to me. It was letting me know who was here and who their allegiance was to. Some of my friends at Auburn were afraid of the gang bangers. Not me! I had become friends of a few Gangster Disciple as well as Vice Lords. Most of the black kids at school were in a gang. I had been around thugs for years, and I knew how to handle myself. To kill the time, I walked in a circle inside of the cell. Maybe the time will go by faster. *How long are they going to keep us in here?*

I lost all track of time. All I kept thinking about was what I was missing at wrestling practice. I wrestled at 112. As one of the smallest and inexperienced guys on the team, one of the upper classmen took me under his wing. Titus was one of my favorites. He was so funny around the guys. Once he was on the mat, he was a different kind of cat. He was all business. At six feet, two inches, and 185 pounds, he was a chiseled athlete. There was no one who could beat him. He won the state championship last year. The reason I liked him so much was because he was so humble.

I had seen Titus around school. He was very popular with all the other kids, especially the girls. During the first practice, Coach Schultz paired him with me. I was lost. I never wrestled before, but a lot of the football players were encouraged to go out for wrestling. Apparently, it was good for building up endurance and increasing balance.

During the first practice, Titus spent extra time on showing me some of the basic moves. After several practices with the team, I finally began to understand the sport, thanks, in a large part to Titus. He had a way of encouraging me. During that first session, he said.

"Look, I was just as lost as you in my freshman year. I was only 110 pounds and clueless. If you try your best and never give up, you will be successful"

That became my mindset as I went into my first match against West. The meet was at West High School. We loaded up into the school bus and made the short trip over to West. I was feeling really excited about this big day. I knew Mom was working and could not be there. I was holding out hope Toots and my brothers would be there to cheer me on. She had always been there for me.

Once I was standing in the locker room with the other guys, I began to get butterflies. I had heard the guys talk about the nervousness of wrestling in their first meet. I was expecting to feel a little nervous, but what I was feeling was much worse than I expected. I was looking on as Coach Schultz was giving us a pep talk. All the sudden, I could feel my lunch coming up. I quietly excused myself from the team meeting in the locker room, moving as fast as I could to the first toilet I saw. The projectile vomit was never ending. Here I was, puking my guts out. How was I going to compete in this kind of shape?

Still in the stall, I heard the team exiting the locker room. I got up and began to walk out of the stall, only to be greeted by my friend Titus.

"Joey, you okay, dude?"

"I am better now, man. I feel really weak."

"Wait here, man."

"Okay," I said. I found a bench to lay down on. The room was still spinning, but at least I didn't have to throw up anymore. Just as I got comfortable Titus reappeared." Sit up, man. Eat these orange slices. It will give you a boost." Without a second thought I sat up and inhaled six orange slices.

"Thank you so much, Titus"

"You are welcome. Look, we need to get out there." I followed Titus out to the gym. The place was packed with fans from both schools. Just as we rejoined our teammates, Titus was called to the center mat. I was watching intently as Titus made quick work of his hapless opponent. He made it look so easy

The oranges really worked. I felt so much better. I began to scan in the stands. I was hoping to see my family here. I didn't see them anywhere. Not content with that reality, I continued to look in vain.

"Joey," came from the bench.

"Get out there; you are up," bellowed Coach Schultz.

I was laser focused. I quickly made my way to the mat. My opponent, although the same weight, looked bigger than me. I was not intimidated. The referee put a blue anklet on me and a red one on my opponent. The whistle blew, and I attacked. I shot a single leg takedown followed by the cradle move. I got him. Just as quickly as it started, it was over. The ref raised my arm in victory. I looked over to my bench; the guys were going nuts.

"Good job, Joey," I heard in unison. What was standing out to me was Titus. He was standing there with a huge smile on his face, clapping for me. I felt like these guys accepted me for me. I was not the fastest, strongest, or quickest. No, I was not any of those things, but I did feel like the luckiest to have these guys as team-mates and friends.

Deep in thought, I was brought back to the here and now by the rattling of a set of keys. I looked to my left to see the jailer unlocking my prison cell.

"Let's go, kid. Time for you to go home." I followed the jailer out of the cell and into the waiting room I was in before. Another door opened—it was Greg!

"Hey, man," he said with a big smile on his face. I was happy to see him.

"Where did they put you, man? I never want to be apart from you again ever!"

"Me, too, Joey. They put me in a little cell. I took a nap." Greg said through his laughter. I could see in his eyes that this little experiment didn't faze him. He had always been a strong kid brother. His will is strong. Always the leader never a follower—that's why I admired him so much.

Another door swung open abruptly. It's Tyrone!

"Greg, come here, boy!" he shouted. I was looking on as Tyrone gave him a hug. He looked over to me during this exchange without saying a word to me. I could see his eyes through those dark lenses. It was a look of pure hatred for me.

"Let's go. Time to go home."

He usually played the radio while driving. Not now. As we pulled into the driveway, he broke the silence.

"Joey, since you decided to run away I have made a decision. You are no longer allowed to be on the wrestling team!" That struck a nerve that the time in jail could not. I couldn't control the flood of tears.

"You know that I enjoy staying active with wrestling. Why are you doing this?"

"I will tell you why when you grow some nuts and tell me why you ran away. I climbed out of the car, crushed but not destroyed. I will never allow him to defeat me.

29
DOWN GOES FRAZIER

On Tuesday after school, I began to walk to Wilson School for wrestling practice with Titus. Suddenly, I remembered Tyrone said I could no longer wrestle. I had been kicked off the team. I was so embarrassed. As I walked along with Titus, I was trying to figure out a way to tell him I was off the team. I didn't have the words as I continued to walk in complete silence. Just as we entered the main entrance, I built up the courage to tell him.

"Hey, man. My stepdad is making me quit the wrestling team."

"Why? You have made so much progress. He must have seen that for himself."

"He has never seen me wrestle. In fact, no one from my family has. Thank you for all your help, man. I have learned so much from you." I didn't want to tell him why. I didn't understand why myself.

"Okay, Joey. See you around, man." I looked on as Titus disappeared in the distance. I turned around and began the long walk home. I felt myself tensing up as the tears began to flow. I was not in a hurry to get home. For what? Just to be relegated to the basement? No, thanks, it was so very cold outside but no worries. I was used to walking in this crap.

As I approached the house, I saw Ronnie's car in the driveway. I picked up the pace. I had not seen him in a long time. He always treated me good. As I entered the house through the back door, I could hear Ronnie talking to someone downstairs. I flew downstairs as I wiped the frozen tears from my face. As I entered the rec room, I saw Ronnie standing there, showing all the boys the sweet science of boxing. Marty, Greg, Leon, and Andre were all intently watching Ronnie as he put on a boxing clinic. Dropping my book bag, I took a seat on the couch and enjoyed the show. He was so fast, so fluid. It reminded me of watching Ali, the heavyweight boxing champ. I really liked boxing. From time to time I would watch boxing with the family. Ali was my favorite. Tyrone was a big fan as well. Those are the only times I could tolerate being around him.

Ronnie was taller but a lot skinner than Tyrone. He had such fast hands. When he finished his clinic, he said, "Leon and Andre, I have a early Christmas gift for you." Ronnie ran upstairs and quickly returned with a big brown paper bag. I was hurt that he didn't have a gift for me. I looked at Greg and Marty. I could tell they were disappointed as well.

As we all looked on, he pulled out two sets of little red boxing gloves. Andre and Leon went crazy with excitement. I jumped up to help Leon put his gloves on. They were too big for him. I laced them up as tight as I could. Now he was ready to go. Ronnie had put on Andre's gloves so fast. I could tell he had done this before.

"Okay, kids, we are going to have a sparring session"

"What is a sparring session, Uncle Ronnie?" Leon asked.

"You guys box each other, Leon," Ronnie said through his laughter.

"Ohhhhhhh," Leon said.

Ronnie walked the boys through a series of drills and techniques before the session started. Although Leon was older, he was not as coordinated as Andre. That became more obvious as they began to pummel each other. Marty and Greg started to look for a chance to put the gloves on.

"Y'all just need to wait your turn. If you guys have good skills, I will be your manager. So, do your best, and do what I tell you."

That got my attention! Tyrone never showed this much interest to any of us, especially me. Now that Andre had given Leon a good beat down, it was Marty and Greg's turn. Greg was really focused as Ronnie put the gloves on him and then helped Marty with his. In a matter of seconds, they were just beating the crap out of each other. I was really surprised. Marty who was the real quiet and reserved brother was getting the best of Greg. Body shot, body shot, left hook. Greg crashed to the floor hard.

"Good job. Go to your corner," Ronnie barked. Marty was happy. He was showboating, taunting,

Ronnie hollered, "Boy, get your pussy butt up. You must be tougher. He barely hit you!" Greg struggled back to his feet.

He looked over to Marty and said, "Let's go again, punk! I am going to kick your butt!"

"Are you sure you want to take another beating, boy?" Marty replied.

"Let's do this," Greg said.

"Okay, boys, come to the center of the ring," Ronnie instructed. Ronnie blew the whistle and Greg was all over Marty. He didn't even throw one punch before Greg knocked him out with a left hook.

"Man, Greg, that was a great effort. Way to bounce back." Ronnie helped Marty back to his feet and removed his gloves.

"That's it for today, boys. I will manage all of you guys. You guys have potential. I need to get home."

"Uncle Ronnie, can I get a turn?" I asked.

"Who are you going to fight, Joey?" he asked.

"Can I fight you?"

"Boy, you have got some balls. The gloves are too small for me. It won't be fair, man."

'That's okay," I said.

I so wanted Ronnie to spend time with me. I mean this was not the ideal way I had envisioned spending time with him. But anytime with him, even boxing against him, was good. I know it was all in fun, anyway.

"Okay, kid. Put your dukes up!"

I was ready. I wanted to show him my boxing skills. Since he was not wearing gloves, I didn't put mine on. Greg blew the whistle, and it was on. I didn't even take one step toward him. He was all over me. Throwing punches from all angles. He was not throwing very hard, but the punches were so fast, I could not properly defend myself. He hit me with a body shot, sending me to the floor. I was doubled over in pain.

"Why did you hit me so hard, man?"

"That was not hard, chump. Man up, pussy!" Marty came over to where I was laying on the floor.

"You okay, Joey? Man, you did a good job!"

"Thanks, I tried."

Marty and Greg were helping me up as I saw Ronnie walking up the stairs. Before he could get to the top of the stairs, I ran over to the bottom of the stairs.

"Ronnie, can you be my manager, too?" I so badly wanted to be a part of this boxing thing.

"Sure, man," he said. I could not wait for his next visit. I wanted him to train me. I will be a great boxer with his help—the next great champion.

We were taking turns boxing each other with the boxing gloves. Then we heard a call from upstairs.

"Y'all come up for dinner." The boys flew up the stairs, knowing the dinner call meant not only food but freedom. I took my time up the stairs. I really dreaded being in his presence.

As I reached the top of the stairs, I made my way to the bathroom. Toots was in there, brushing her hair.

"Hey, Toots, how are you doing? Did you just get home?"

"I am okay, Joey. No, I was in my room doing my homework."

"Oh. Did you see Ronnie before?"

"Only for a minute when I got home from school," she said as she continued to brush her hair "Joey, go get some dinner. I cooked hotdogs."

"Okay, man."

I felt myself getting real tense as I walked into the kitchen. Tyrone was standing at the kitchen sink. He had his big cup of brandy on the counter next to him. I sat down to eat a hotdog with the family. I was hungry before, but I have lost my appetite. Marty, Greg, Leon, and Andre were really chowing down, oblivious to my presence. Toots walked into the kitchen and joined us for dinner.

Between sips of his brandy, Tyrone asked questions.

"What did you guys think about boxing?"

Marty was the first to respond.

"It was so much fun. Uncle Ronnie is a good boxer."

"Yes he is, but I am better," he said, matter of fact.

"Hurry up and finish dinner. I will show you boys even more tricks."

"Yay," the boys said in unison. I was not interested in what he wanted to show us. I mean he was drunk. I hated to be around him when he was drinking. The boys finished eating and ran into the study. Tyrone walked in behind them and instructed them to sit down. Even Toots got up and walked into the study. Here I was at the table by myself. With no one around, I quickly jumped up and throw my paper plate of food into the garbage. As I began to walk down the stairs, I heard a shout.

"Boy, get back up here. Who told you to go downstairs?"

Crap! He heard me. I was frozen with fear. Whatever he wanted, I had the sense that it was not good. He had a habit of singling me out. I felt my heart really racing now as I climbed back up the stairs and into his study. All the boys were sitting on the couch, waiting for Tyrone to put on his clinic, I guess. I didn't want to sit down. I just stood there by the entryway, staring at the ground. I was afraid to look at him.

"You, boy! Take off your shirt" he bellowed.

Take off my shirt? Okay this was getting weird fast! I reluctantly took off my shirt. I stole a glance in his direction. Tyrone was sitting on his chair facing me. With his trusty alcoholic drink in his hand, he began.

"When you throw a punch, boys, you need to throw the punch from the shoulder. This way the punch has a more powerful effect." I looked over at my brothers as they sat quietly listening to all of this with real interest.

"I will demonstrate. Joey, stand in front of me." With my head still down, I walked to where he was sitting. I could see his feet, so I knew I was standing in front of him.

"Boy! Look at me! Now I am going to punch you in the chest. Then I want you to punch me back. Punch me right in the chest. Remember to throw from the shoulder."

I nodded my head and braced myself for the punch. *Boom!* Tyrone punched me in the chest. He punched me so hard I fell backward.

"Now your turn!" I was so afraid. My heart was going to burst out of my chest at any second.

Things got more nerve wracking when the kids started to chant, "Do it. Do It."

I took my eyes off him for a second. I saw Toots standing in the other doorway facing me. She had a look of sympathy for me on her face. I returned my gaze on Tyrone as I throw my first punch.

"Boy, grow some balls and punch me, you sissy! That was a slap. Throw from your shoulder, pussy!"

This time I studied his chest. He was a huge man, much bigger than Ronnie, and he hit a lot harder. I took a deep breath and launched my punch.

"That was pathetic."

"Stand still I will show you one more time!" I braced myself as Tyrone punched me. He hit me much harder this time. I lost my balance and fell backward toward the TV. I hit my head on the corner of the TV. I screamed from the top of my lungs. It hurt so badly.

"Get your bitch ass up, sissy!" Tyrone barked. I could feel the blood flowing down the side of my face and into my mouth now.

Once I got my bearings, I struggled to my feet and walked out of the room. I reached to the back of my head to feel the wound. Why does he continue to treat me like crap? He didn't even come check on me. Toots came into the kitchen and inspected my injury. She was so nurturing.

"I am going to get you an ice pack, man. Go downstairs." She didn't have to tell me twice. I made my way to my room and laid down on my bed. Toots walked into my room with a huge ice pack. As she placed it on the wound, I asked, "Why did he do that, Toots? He is always picking on me. He was hitting me hard."

"I don't know, man. Stay strong. Don't let him destroy your spirit, man." I looked on as she exited my room. Once I heard her walking up the stairs, I began to cry uncontrollably. God, why are you letting this happen to me?

30
FREE TO RUN

I just finished my last day of school in ninth grade. I was so pumped to be done I couldn't wait to see Dad this summer. I walked home quicker than normal. If I just meditated on my family in Dubuque, I could get through the next few days of being around Tyrone. In the evening after dinner, Tyrone summoned all of us to the living room. Everyone was there except for Mom. She was at work.

"Okay, I want to let you all know that there will be no vacation in Dubuque. We have things we need to get done around here. So, if you had hopes of going, you can forget that crap." The room went silent for what seemed like forever before Marty spoke up, "Why can't I go, Dad?" he asked timidly as he pushed his glasses back onto his nose.

"I don't feel any of you have earned a vacation," he responded as he looked at me. Now I got it. This was payback to me and Greg for running away. Not only did he force me to quit the wrestling team. He just dropped a bomb on me. I didn't really care if he thought I earned to go or not. He was not my dad. He was a waste of space at most. I found the courage and blurted out," I am going to ask Mom. She will let me go."

"Hey boy! I have made the decision, and your mommy can't change it. Deal with it! This meeting is over. You boys go play outside." I led the pack outside through the kitchen and out the back door. I quickly found the football in the backyard and threw a tight spiral to Marty, who was sprinting toward the fence by the alley. He was small for his age but both fast and agile.

"Let's pick teams, Joey," Greg shouted as he ran by. He was running after Marty, but he couldn't catch up to him. He was way too fast. They finally made it by the back door.

"Okay, Marty and I are captains. You pick first, Marty."

"Okay, I pick, Andre." Darn I wanted him.

"Okay, Leon, I got you, man." I said. There was Toots and Greg left. I should have picked her before Leon.

"I pick Toots," Marty replied. Greg was the only one left.

"I saved the best for last. Greg, come on!" Now that the teams were chosen, my team lined up to kick off. We had played football countless times in the backyard. It was like second nature to me. I felt like all was good with my world when I was spending time this way.

Just as we were ready to start, Tyrone walked outside through the back door. Leon ran up to him.

"Dad can you be quarterback all the time?" Everyone was clamoring for the same thing. Not me! I didn't want him playing with us.

"Sure, I got time." My kid brothers were jumping up and down with excitement. With that late addition, I was taking myself out. I walked over to the garage to grab my bike.

"Hey where are you going, Joey?" Toots asked.

"Going for a bike ride, man." Tyrone interjected.

"No, you are not. If you can't play football, you can go to your room! Everyone else is playing. Why can't you?" I jumped off my bike and walked it back into the garage. I quickly reemerged, carful to not look at him. I walked with my head down as I entered the house and made my way to my room.

I laid on my bed feeling less tense now that I was away from him. I could hear the kids playing out there. It sounded like they were having fun. I stared at the ceiling, thinking about what I could be doing if I was in Dubuque. This was a good time to take a nap. I could feel my eyes getting heavy. The sleep came quickly.

Now that I was not allowed to travel to Dubuque during the summer months, I got the sense that Tyrone was going to make life even more difficult for me. I asked Mom if I could go, but she told me no. He had her wrapped around his little finger.

Ever since I ran away, Tyrone had become even more unloving toward me if that was even possible. I wouldn't give him the satisfaction. I would never show him my true emotions. I was now confident he would do everything in his power to dispose of me. The summer was going by fast. I was given the grass-cutting responsibility. I didn't mind. I really didn't. I loved to be outside.

I liked to stay busy. When I was not riding my bike, playing football with my brothers. I enjoyed cleaning the downstairs living area. No matter how much I did around the house to help, it was never good enough for them. Whenever I would do something to make them angry. I would be reminded of the promise they made.

"We don't want you. You will be going to live in a foster home." The thought running through my head when they would bring it up was, *Yeah, whatever. I am tired of hearing the crap. Pull the trigger and do it. It can't be as dysfunctional as this family.* Deep inside, I was crushed. I was crying inside and on the verge of totally giving up. Maybe I should do them a favor and end my life. That thought flooded my mind daily. It was 8 a.m. when I woke up. I looked over at Marty's bed. His bed was made flawlessly as usual, but I was not sure where he was. He was probably eating breakfast with Toots and the boys. I quickly threw my bed together. Once I got dressed, I walked into Greg, Leon, and Andre's adjoining room. None of those guys were around, either. It was odd to not hear them making a racket. As I walked upstairs, all I heard was silence. There on the kitchen table was a note from Toots.

"We went to Page Park. See you later." I liked going to Page Park. Why didn't they wake me up? I walked out to the garage to see if they took their bikes. All the bikes were in the garage, but the car was gone. I guess the whole family was together.

I returned to the kitchen and prepared a bowl of cereal. All I was thinking about was what fun they must be having. They were doing it without me! I finished breakfast and headed back downstairs. That would not have been a big deal if it was the first time something like that had happened. The fact is that it was not. Many times, I was left out. I knew it wasn't my siblings' fault. I blamed Mom and Tyrone. I tuned the TV on to see if there were any cartoons on. I came across a story about the Chicago Bears Football Team.

They were my favorite team by far. I began to watch the documentary, but the thought of the family going without me began to build. I couldn't stop the tears from flowing. *Do they really plan on getting rid of me? They want me gone for sure. I will help them with that.* I began to have thoughts of ending my life again. *That will fix them.* I was sitting on the basement stairs frozen in place as I thought of ways to end my life. I mean Dad was never going to rescue us. My huge extended family didn't do anything other than to threaten "bodily harm" to Tyrone. No one had ever followed through. The fact was, everyone was afraid of him, and frankly they didn't want to get involved.

Tyrone had a .38-caliber handgun. He carried it on him in a shoulder harness. Often, he would have one of the kids help him to put the harness on. He had such broad shoulders. He found it difficult to get it on by himself. If I could somehow get to the gun, I could solve everyone's woes. They can deal with the aftermath. I will be at peace; I was sure of that. I decided to go look for the gun. I walked into their bedroom. I was looking high and low for the gun, being ever so carful as to not move things around too much. I couldn't let them know I was in their room. I continued to look everywhere I thought it could be, but no luck.

I heard the car pull into the driveway. Crap, I was going to get caught.' I ran as fast as I could out of their room through the study and down the stairs. I resumed watching TV. I didn't want anyone to think I was upset about them going without me. Andre and Leon came barreling down the stairs, followed by Marty and then Greg.

"Hey, Joey," Greg said excitedly.

"Man, the park was awesome. You should have been there, man. I caught a huge snake."

"Awesome! Where is it?"

"Ma made me let it go. She said we have nowhere to put it."

"Oh well, that sucks, man"

"Yeah, we had so much fun, man. Wish you were with us," Marty said.

"Me, too, man, me too," I said. Andre and Leon ran directly into their bedroom and then back up the stairs. Greg and Marty followed them as I looked on. I followed them upstairs and out the back door. They were all getting back into the car. Tyrone was behind the wheel. Mom was in the passenger seat. Toots and the boys were fighting over the middle seat in the back. I hollered.

"Where are you guys going, Mom?"

"We are going to see Gail. We will be back soon." I just turned around and headed back to the basement. It was clear to me now. I was just in the way. I guess out of sight out of mind.

It was dark when the family returned. As soon as Mom opened the basement door, I could tell by the way she was staggering that she was drunk. I stood at the bottom of the stairs as she struggled to stay upright as she descended the stairs.

Yelling at the top of her lungs, she got closer, "You little son of a bitch. I am putting you on the phone with your grandparents. Maybe they will take you! I am sick and tired of your crap!"

She was two inches from my face. Her eyes were bloodshot, and her breath smelled terrible. It was a combination of cigarettes and alcohol. I was standing there perfectly still as she continued to rip into me.

"I will put you on the first bus in the morning, you moron. Go over to the phone. We are going to call your Grandma. She loves you so much, huh? Well, she can have you."

I began to walk over to the phone. She was walking right behind me. She did not like the fact that I was walking slowly with my head down. *What did she want from me?* She grabbed a handful of my hair in the back of my head and yanked my head back toward her.

"Get moving, you simpleton!" Once at the phone, she released the vice-grip hold she had on my hair. I stood there crying uncontrollably. I was afraid to look at her. I continued to stare at the ground as I heard her dial the number. I could hear the other end ringing, and then I heard a familiar voice. It was Tyrone.

"June, you talk to them. I will just listen. If they get ignorant, I will speak up."

"Okay," was all she said. The phone continued to ring. It was late. I knew they were probably in bed. Mom spoke up.

"They are in bed, Tyrone. I am going to hang up." I was still staring at the ground, hoping they didn't answer. As Mom began to hang up the receiver, a faint voice came from the other end.

"Hello, who is this?" Grandma asked. 'Oh, boy, here we go."

She returned the receiver to her ear and started her rant.

"We are wondering if you will take Joey." She was slurring her words so bad. I was sure Grandma didn't understand her.

"June, why are you calling me so late?"

"I am sorry. It is just we are running out of patience with Joey."

"June, we had this conversation before if you remember. We love Joey. In fact, we love all your children, but we are just too old to raise him. I am sorry." I could hear every word. I was crushed.

"Well, here he is. You tell him that you don't want him." Mom put the phone in my hand and demanded I talk to Grandma. I pulled the receiver to my ear. I could hear Tyrone on the other end. He was breathing heavy.

"Hi Grandma. Can I please come there, please?"

"Hi, honey. We love you very much. We are just too old to raise another child." I swallowed really hard. Fighting back the wave of tears, I mustered the words.

"I love you, too." I was so devastated now. I looked at Mom as I handed her the receiver. She had a look of pure hatred in her eyes for me. She stuck her index finger in my face.

"Go to bed, you creep!"

I got into my bed and crawled under my blankets. Marty was still awake. I didn't want him to see that I was crying. I covered my head up with the blankets and somehow drifted off to sleep.

31
TAKING IT FOR THE TEAM

Tenth grade was well underway. I couldn't wait for wrestling season to start. I was very surprised Tyrone and Mom allowed me to sign up for wrestling again. After all, he forced me to quit after I ran away. Coach Schultz was one of the few men I looked up to. I was so excited to once again wrestle for him.

Once the wrestling practices began, I felt at ease, even when I had to go against more experienced teammates. I tried to beat them, but I would usually get my butt kicked on the mat by the more seasoned guys. I took all of this in stride. It was a part of the learning process.

I put all my effort into this sport. I really wanted to be the best I could. I didn't need any support from home. They have never truly cared about my endeavors.' I was fine with that. I was doing this for me! I loved this team environment in which I could grow and learn. I hated it when I had to return home each night after practice because there was always a battle going on.

After one very hard, tough practice, I began to walk home along Auburn Street. Rockford was being pummeled by a blizzard. I was hoping Tyrone would get off his butt, and come get me, but that was wishful thinking. As I walked past the tennis courts on the corner of Auburn and Pierpont, I heard a vehicle honk behind me. I turned to see Coach Schwartz behind the wheel of his van, waving for me to get in.

I walked back to the passenger side when one of the varsity wrestlers and the coach greeted me.

"Where you are heading Joey?"

"Shelley Drive."

"Get in; I am heading that way."

"Thank you so very much, Coach!" As we got near Auburn Manor, Coach said.

"How about I drop you off here in front of Auburn Manor?"

"That would be great, thanks." It was a very short walk from there. That became a routine after every practice. Usually, we would talk about wrestling and what I needed to improve on. Whenever he would ask about home, I would change the subject. He was very nice. I was not used to people showing random acts of kindness. I often thought, *"There must be a catch."*

As I arrived home, I braced myself as I entered the zone. Ma was at work, and I spied him sitting in the study with his huge cup of brandy.

"Your dinner is on the table, eat and hit it." I ate the chicken and dumplings as fast as I could. I quickly cleaned up my dinner dishes and headed down to my room. As I changed into my pajamas, I could not help but wonder where Dad was. It had been a while since I had seen him. I wondered if he heard about Mom trying to convince my grandparents to take me in. If he knew, would he come? Will he finally man up and get his family back? I laid in bed with these thoughts flooding my mind. Please, Dad, wherever you are, come save us from this nightmare!

Shelter

With December now here, I noticed a change with Ma. She began telling me and Toots that she was going to leave Tyrone. She would usually tell us while she was drinking at home when he was away.

"Don't be surprised if you get yanked out of school someday. I am leaving that ape." We both have heard this all before. This time was different. What started off as a drunken rant soon became a daily reminder.

I was at wrestling practice on a Wednesday evening when I saw Coach Schultz walking right over to where I was going through my stretch exercises.

"Joey, come with me!" Coach was always smiling and joking around but not now. He had a serious look on his face. I followed him out into the hallway. I could feel my heart beating a million miles an hour. All these thoughts began to flood my mind. *Is Coach Schultz cutting me from the team? Did I break some rule? My grades are above average, so I know I am eligible to wrestle for Auburn.* By the time I reached the hallway, I was sweating profusely.

"I got a phone call from your mom. She needs you to come home right away," Coach said in a calm, measured tone.

The room began to spin out of control. I quickly changed back into my street clothes and got home as fast as I could. I never knew what to expect when I entered the hellhole; this time was no exception. I got home just in time for dinner.

"Joey, you got dishes tonight." Tyrone reminded me as we all ate around the dinner table. I could tell something major was about to happen. Mom was home on a weeknight. Unusal. After dinner, Tyrone left the house, which was his routine. I was at the kitchen sink when Mom came running into the kitchen.

"Grab some clothes, we are leaving."

Before I ran downstairs, Mom grabbed the kitchen phone. She was having trouble dialing the number.

"Mom, what is the number? I will dial it." I ran up next to her and grabbed the receiver out of her hand. She was shaking so hard. I considered her eyes and seen the look of complete fear. She managed to read off the phone number to me from the phonebook as she dragged on her beloved cigarette. The other end began to ring.

"Here, Ma, it's ringing." She took a deep drag from her cancer stick as she took the receiver. I looked on as Mom hollered into the phone.

"Our lives are in danger. My husband has threatened to kill my kids and me. I want to leave him. I need the cops here now! Mom paused as she listened to the person on the other end.

"No, you heard me correctly! I need you to send a bunch of cops here. He is crazy, and he has a gun." She took her attention away from the phone call long enough to look at me with a panicked look.

"Go grab some clothes, moron!" I heard enough from the call that I knew Mom was serious. This was really happening. I flew down to my room and grabbed whatever clothes I could. I heard Greg and the other boys in their room. Running as fast as I could, I went into the room and helped the boys pack their bags. Leon and Andre were crying. They didn't understand what was going on. I could see Marty was sitting on Leon's bed, trying to console him. All the sudden, Andre ran up to me.

"Where are we going? Is Dad coming, too, Joey?"

"Not this time. Don't worry; everything will be fine. You will see."

Whatever Marty said to Leon seemed to have helped. I was so nervous. Tyrone could return at any time. This process was taking way too long. I looked over to Greg, who was still stuffing random clothes into a laundry basket.

"Okay we have to go guys." Marty took Leon and Andre upstairs to get their coats on. Greg thought he needed more things from his dresser because he pretended not to hear me. He was throwing random junk into the basket.

"Hey man! Do you want out of this prison, or do you want to stay? If we don't get a move on, Tyrone is going to catch us trying to leave." He looked up at me. I could see the look he was giving me.

"We ain't getting caught, man." As we made it into the kitchen, I heard a car pull up in the driveway. My heart fell to my feet as I froze in place with fear, nervousness, and utter dread.

Mom was pacing back and forth in the kitchen. I could see she had smoked the whole pack of smokes she had been clutching in her hand. I was afraid to see who was in the driveway. I could tell she was, too. Just then Toots appeared out of her room and made a beeline to the front door. She wasted no time swinging open the door to see if Tyrone had returned or if indeed the police had arrived.

"Let's go," she blurted out. She had a big bag in her arm. With one motion, she walked over to Andre and picked him up and ran out to the cop car. Marty, Greg, and Leon were running right behind her. I ran out to the car behind Marty. Just as we all got crammed into the car, Mom ran up to the driver side of the police car. The cop rolled down his window.

"Where in the hell are the other cops?" Mom barked at the officer.

"Ma'am I am the only unit available. Now if you can, step away from the car, so I can get out."

"Well, if Tyrone shows up, you will need the whole department. He is crazy!" I was thinking the same thing. In fact, I was convinced he would return at any moment. This all seemed too easy.

Mom backed away from the car as the officer exited.

"I am responding to your phone call. I understand your desire to leave now. However, I need to file a report. Can we step inside the house to talk in private?" I wanted to scream, "You don't understand. If he comes back and catches us, we are all in danger." Mom screamed. She reluctantly led the officer into the house.

Finally, Mom and the cop returned to the car. The cop backed out of the drive and began to drive off

We did not know what to expect when we drove up to this big asbestos brick house, sitting on a big lot downtown. It looked worn out, but any place will do if it meant being away from him. I was hoping Mom would be different, too. She had been so hard to deal with.

The cop took Mom into the front of the house while we all stayed in the car. It seemed like forever before she returned.

"Okay, kids, grab something to carry in. We will go into the house through the back door."

As soon as we walked into the house, we were greeted by a big black woman.

"Hello all, my name is Patsy. I am one of the staff members here. I will be here every night. Follow me, and I will show you your living arrangements." We followed her, through the house. *Boy, this place is a far cry from the house we were living in.* During the tour, the number of people living there surprised me. I guess I didn't expect all of this. All I knew was we were free from Tyrone, hopefully forever. At the end of the hallway was the bathroom that we all must share.

After the tour, Patsy turned to us with a big beautiful smile. Instantly, the anxiety I had up until that point dissipated. I couldn't help but notice that she had a big gold front tooth. I could also see in her eyes that she loved to help people. She was here to help and not hurt me. For that I was grateful.

With her country drawl, Patsy announced, "I want to welcome you all. It's lights out! See you in the morning." I made a beeline to my room. Marty and Greg were on my heels as we made it up the squeaky stairs and into the room. I noticed the lights were out. I could see silhouettes of other kids asleep on their beds. From the corner of my eye, I saw Marty reaching for the light switch on the wall.

"Marty, don't turn it on. I don't want to wake them up. Just find a bed to sleep on." I looked on as Marty and Greg each claimed a bed for the night. I stumbled around in the pitch-black room, finally finding a twin-size bed. I was so tired. I jumped under the blankets. I was starring at the ceiling as I reviewed what took place tonight. I couldn't believe we got away! *When I wake up, will I wake up on Shelley Drive? Was this all a dream? Will I be awakened to Tyrone hollering at Ma or beating her senseless?* All these thoughts flooded my mind as I laid there among my brothers in this new place. Tomorrow promised to be even longer as we still need to get adjusted to our new home—the shelter.

32
YOU CAN RUN, BUT YOU CAN'T HIDE!

I got into a good sleep when I was awakened by one of the staff members. She instructed us to come down for breakfast. After breakfast, we were told to meet in the office to go over more house rules. After the meeting, Ma informed me that she had to go to the police station to file an order of protection against Tyrone. She wanted me to go with her. I could tell she was scared. She was inhaling cigarette after cigarette as she led the way to the police station.

My head was on a swivel as I looked for any sign of him. The station was only a few blocks from the shelter. We were walking fast, but it seemed like it was taking forever to get there.

Just as we arrived, Tyrone pulled up in the passenger seat of his friend's yellow pickup. I exchanged stares with him. It looked like he was about to launch out of the cab right toward me. I managed to stare right through his dark lenses into his eyes. He had a look of disdain and hate for me. I noticed he was clinching his jaw muscles. When he did that, I knew he was about to do something. I had never stared Tyrone down like that before. If he could read my mind, he would know that *I am free from you! You lose*! I broke my stare and went inside. I saw Mom at the desk, talking to the police.

I struggled with the idea. How was a piece of paper going to keep him from getting to Mom? He was crazy. He had proven that again and again. I believed the cops were afraid of him as well by how they acted when His name came up. I was just a kid, but I could see the cop's uneasiness when it came to dealing with him.

After she signed all the paperwork, we peeked outside to ensure we didn't see Tyrone around. Although he had seen us, I was hoping he didn't see us walking from the shelter because if he did, I knew we were in for a long day. Mom didn't say one word on the way home. She was as white as a ghost, but once we got into the shelter, she became more relaxed, and that made it easier for all of us.

Being in the battered woman shelter was very hard. We went from having our own space to having to share everything, including household chores. I guess that was to teach us teamwork, *and* appreciate what we had.

Mom kept all of us kids out of school until after Christmas break. The staff at the shelter was kind enough to pick up all our materials and homework. They did that, I guess, because Ma knew Tyrone would probably show up at the schools to look for us. Even though there was a court order for him to stay away, I knew better. It was only a matter of time before he found out where we were hiding. Then he will force Ma to move back home. I have been down that road before, and I was still very uneasy in the new settings. After Christmas break, it was determined that we should return to school.

Once I got to the school, I made my way to Mr. Trap's class. I barely got my book out of my bag when Al the school cop came into the room. He whispered something to Mr. Trap, and they then called me into the hallway. As I walked into the hallway, I could feel every eye in the room on me. I had never seen Al look so distraught. He was always so laid back and relaxed. He always seemed to have everything under control; something was up. They turned their attention to me as I stood in front of them.

"Joey, you need to pack up your things."

"Why?"

"Son, I will explain later," Al offered. I didn't understand what was going on.

"What is going on, what happened to my Mom?" I blurted out. Tyrone must have gotten to her and did something to her. He promised he would kill her if she left him again." I was scared to death as I waited for a response.

"Joey, Tyrone was seen driving onto school property. We need to see you and your sister off the premises."

"And go where exactly? Tyrone carries a gun; he is crazy!"

"Don't worry about him; we have a squad car waiting for you in the front of the building. You and your sister will be fine."

Under control was something these cops were not. They feared Tyrone. Even Al was shaking in his boots. I had seen it hundreds of times with other people when it came to dealing with Tyrone. He was so intimidating.

Before I knew it, Toots and I were sitting in the back of the squad car going nowhere. I didn't know what the holdup was. Did they want us to wave goodbye to him or what? Finally, the cop returned to the car and off we went.

As we drove down Auburn Street, I looked back at the school at the swarm of cop cars, trying to see if I could see Tyrone. After all, he was trespassing in a sense. I didn't see any sign of Tyrone. Was he in the back of one of the cars? That made me that much more uneasy. I remember some years ago, the scuffle he got into with the cops in his mom's front yard. He was not afraid of the cops at all, but they were terrified of him. That was killing me inside. Once he found us, what could they do? They seemed like a bunch of bumbling idiots.

We didn't say a word the whole ride back to the shelter. I figured that was where we were heading. I just had a gut feeling Tyrone will now know where we were living. There was no stopping him, but maybe he would back off once he realized Mom was seriously not going back this time. At least, that was what she kept telling everyone. I didn't believe it. I thought Toots was very skeptical as well.

Before I knew it, we were back in the shelter, reunited with the other kids. The boys didn't seem too phased by the action (or drama) over the last several weeks. I thought we had all gotten a little tougher—emotionally. That was a requirement if we were going to get through this mess.

St. Peter's Church was still the brightest spot in my life. The following Sunday, Ma called the church and informed them where to pick us up. After we ran away, Tyrone forced us to attend his childhood church. He would never go. Often, he would pick us up but never once set foot in the church.

I was embarrassed as I walked to the church van on that first Sunday at the shelter. For months now, I had been outdone by the other people there. They all dressed in the finest clothes. We just had rags in comparison, but I tried not to let that bother me. I was excited that Mom was going with us. God knew we all needed time in His house. I had been so ready to get out for some time. We couldn't leave the shelter unless it was for official business or school. It was like a jail. No man was allowed in the building, period. This was to protect the people inside from a distraught husband or boyfriend.

At the church, everything was the same. There were a couple of families that offered to help us during our transition. The fact remained that we needed to find our own place within ninety days; those were the shelter rules. I had no idea what Mom had in the works, but I had learned time doesn't stop for anyone.

After about a month of living in the shelter, the church informed mom a long-time tenant moved out of a church-owned property, and they would be willing to rent it to us. Mom jumped at the chance to go look at it. It was in the evening when Mr. and Mrs. Jackson, an elderly couple from the church, picked us up to check out the apartment. It was a light brown asbestos brick apartment building. It looked rough.

We entered through the front door and were given a tour of the place. Yep, just as I thought, it was a real dump. It had paneling on the walls, old appliances, and roaches.

After Mom walked through it one time, she said, "I want it. It had four bedrooms, it was on the bus line, and there was a big yard." It didn't matter what her kids thought. We knew we had to leave the shelter. The church agreed to rent to us and worked with Mom on the rent. Over the next few days, we moved in. Wigton was going to be our new home. For me, I was hoping it was going to be a fresh start with Mom. I loved her so much.

33
BIG BROTHER

No matter how hard I tried to be the big brother, it was never good enough. One day after school I came home to find a guy sitting in the front room talking to Ma. He was a big muscular guy with dark hair and glasses.

"Joey this is Mark. He is going to be Marty and Greg's big brother." He stood up as Ma introduced him.

"Hi, Joey, nice to meet you."

"Thanks, nice to meet you, too." My head began to spin with a ton of emotions. I walked back to my bedroom. Collapsing on my bed, I was hurt to the core. First, why did she go get a big brother without including the rest of us? She never told me and Toots her plans. She just did it. She reminded me daily of what a failure I was, and it was getting old. As I laid in bed, I could hear Mark talking to Marty and Greg as they walked pass my room and out the front door. They loaded up in his car and took off. I walked into the kitchen where I fiound Ma sitting at the table smoking a cigarette.

"Joey, you know if you were not such a piece of crap, I would not have needed to ask for help from Big Brothers. It is because of you, this is going on!"

Here we go again, I thought to myself.

"How is it my fault!?" I screamed back at her. In a flash, she jumped up from the table and began to pummel me. I could easily overpower her or just hold her but after seeing her beaten by the hand of Tyrone for years, I guess I didn't want to see her hurt. It was over in a matter of seconds. Content with her handiwork, she stormed off to her bedroom. I just stood there in the corner of the kitchen overwhelmed with emotion. The beating did not hurt, but the words cut to the core. How was it my fault? Why was she blaming me for everything even after we left him?

I need an answer to that question. After a few moments, I could smell the all-too-familiar stench of weed coming from her bedroom. I knocked on the door as I walked in. She was sitting on her bed getting high.

"Just tell me, how is this my fault?"

"Joey, that ape hates you, He wanted me to get rid of you for years. You know that! I was beaten to dust *because of it*! I took a lot of crap from him! I could see in her eyes nothing but pure hate—the same hate Tyrone displayed.

"And it is my fault that *the boys have issues*? How can you blame me for that?" I asked sincerely.

After a long pause and Mom sucking the life out of the joint, she said, "Joey, you need to be a father and a brother to these boys, but once again, you failed. You can't do anything right!"

Without saying another word, I turned around and went back to my room. Scarred both physically and emotionally, I was deflated. I had never had a male role model to look up to other than my grandpa and yet she expected me to be this perfect big brother and father figure to fatherless kids. I didn't understand.

The Big Brothers and Sisters Organization was a very good program. I was glad my brothers had an adult man in their lives who could help them. But the way in which Mom set the stage and filled Mark in with her twisted agenda was wrong. I overheard her telling Mark that I was a failure as a big brother. I thought he believed her because whenever he came to pick up Marty and Greg, he treated me like crap. I mean just very cold and indifferent. Mom had a way of manipulating people, and it looked like she had him in her hip pocket.

34
SOMEONE TO LOOK UP TO

In the spring of my sophomore year I heard that North West Community Center needed assistant baseball coaches. I was sixteen now. I thought I was old enough to get involved. There were flyers all over the school hallways, and they got my attention. I went through the proper channels, and with the green light from Mom, who could care less, I was all in. After the background check and interview by the director, I was assigned to the White Sox.

Stan escorted me and the handful of other new coaches to the gym. There I was introduced to Tommy and Robert.

Tommy was the head coach. He, as well as the other coach, were big black dudes. Tommy was every part six feet, six inches, and 220 pounds. Robert was even taller. If I must guess, he was carrying 400 pounds on his frame. That didn't bother me at all. The fact that Tommy and Robert were huge men may intimidate some but not me.

Other than teaching my kid brothers what I knew about ball. I never really had any experience with coaching. I just knew I wanted to make a difference in the kids' lives here. If that was possible through baseball,

After the meet and greet with all the other coaches, I walked up to the bus stop to get home. To my surprise, Tommy drove up to me.

"Hey, Joey where do you live? I will give you a ride."

"I live on the south side by Eagle's."

"Oh, so do I. Get in." Tommy agreed to drop me off after games and practices. It was really a big deal to me because I was not accustomed to random acts of kindness like that. Robert was nothing like Tommy. He was the other assistant coach. I noticed during the very first practice, he was belittling the guys and was not very nice. I mean, not once did I see any good come out of him hollering and yelling at the kids. He reminded me of Tyrone. During the next practice, I was working on batting practice with the players. Robert walked up to home plate and once again tore into one of the players for not being "tough enough." I wanted to confront him on how he treated the kids, but I was not the boss. Tommy was.

In spite of him, I pressed on. I assisted Tommy in every way possible. I wanted everyone to have a chance. Even if it meant I stayed longer and caught the bus home instead of riding with Tommy, I was after all, here for the kids.

After the second practice, Tommy informed me.

"Joey you are our first-base coach. You have earned that spot. You are great with the kids."

"Thanks, Coach!" *I am the first-base coach instead of Robert?* I thought to myself. I was so shocked.

"I won't let you down, Tommy! I will do my very best."

"I know you will, son. Good job!" As I was working with Stan with his fielding skills, I saw Robert watching us. There he was puffing on a cheap cigar, staring right through me. *Ha,* I thought. *That's all you got? Seriously? You must be kidding. My mom puts the fear of God in me and you? You just make me laugh. Don't you have something you should be doing with the other kids?* I thought to myself.

The sad thing was, over time I discovered most of the kids didn't have a dad at home or another male role model who would work with them. I wanted to be that for them, and I would take extra time with them. I guess because I wanted them to try their best, leave it all when they are on the field, and feel good about themselves.

35
WAR PATH

W e only had a six-week season, and what a season it was. We went undefeated, winning the championship! We had been informed six short weeks ago that the winning team got a big prize—a trip to a Chicago White Sox game. The fact that we were the White Sox, made it that much more special that we won. The Center put on a potluck the next day. After the meal, Stan Johnson went through the list of winning teams based on age group.

Finally, he got to the nine-to-ten-year-old class.

"It gives me great pleasure to announce the next team. I have watched these kids grow and mature into a good baseball team. The White Sox, please come forward. I stayed at the back of the room. I did't feel worthy of any of this. I watched as Tommy accepted the huge trophy. Once the thunderous applause died down, he spoke into the mic." I want to thank the Center, Stan, and the parents for giving me this opportunity. None of this would have been possible without all of you. I had a couple of good coaches on this team. They are a huge part of our success." I was starting to feel nervous now. *Please don't call me up there, please*! Tommy was up there behind the podium scanning the crowd. Was he looking for me? Robert was up there taking it all in. I don't want to go in front of all those parents. Sweating now, I bolted out of the room and into the bathroom. I could hear Tommy call my name.

"Joey, come up with the team." I paced back and forth in the bathroom countless times.

After a couple minutes, I could hear people walking past the bathroom. I made my way back out into the hallway. There I saw Tommy walking to his car. I ran as fast as I could to his car. I really wanted a ride today. As we began the trip home, Tommy was quiet. That was not like him. He usually talked my ear off. Of all days to be quiet, I didn't expect him to clam up like this. As Tommy pulled into the driveway at the apartment, he broke the silence.

"Joey, I know it must be hard for you and your family. I know your mom struggles to make ends meet. I want to help. You know the kids go for free. We as the coaches must pay. I don't think it is fair. But it is what it is. I will pay for you to go with us to Chicago. You are a part of the team, Joey. Everyone is going. I think the boys will be sad if you don't go with us."

"You don't need to do that. I will ask my mom. Maybe she can afford for me to go. I will call you tomorrow."

"No, Joey, you need to let me know tonight. We have to turn in the count first thing in the morning."

"Okay, I will call you tonight." As I looked on, Tommy backed out of the driveway and out of sight, my heart sank. Mom never had enough money to pay bills, not to mention the fact that we hardly ever have enough food. It was funny. Mom had money to buy cigarettes, booze, and weed but not much else.

Mom had been irate lately. Leon and Andre ran away to be with their dad a couple days ago. That became a routine with Leon. He had been getting into fights with Greg. Naturally, Andre took his side so at some point they called their dad, and as I found out later, he picked them up at Eagles, the local grocery store just down the street. Mom had primary custody of the boys, but until this point, Tyrone had not helped her with child support of any kind. I thought that made her irate all the time. Mom couldn't afford for the boys to play ball down at the center. Even after pleading with her, it was no use. I thought it would be very good for them. Whenever I would ask about the boys playing for the center, she would always say, "I don't have the money. That ape doesn't pay me a dime, Joey. How can I afford it?"

"Can't you talk to the coaches to let them play for free?"

"No, it's not up to the coaches." It was just a waste of time even talking to her about anything nowadays, especially this issue. It was like talking to the wall.

I walked through the front door and was surprised to see that she seemed to be in a good mood.

"Hi, Mom. I have some good news! Since we won the championship game yesterday, there is a trip to Chicago for the team. It costs fifty dollars. Do you think I can go?"

"How are you going to get the money, huh? Do you expect me to pull it out of thin air, you moron? Get out of my face, dummy. Even if I had the money, I would not give to you for the trip. You don't deserve it! I should have let Grace adopt your years ago, but now I am stuck with you. Don' ask me for anything, you little bastard!" I was shocked she didn't knock me around a little bit. At least the injuries will heal but not her words "Tommy said if you could not pay, he would. I need to call him tonight and tell him if I am going or not."

"Yeah, call him. Inform him that you can't go!"

"Why? He will pay my way!" She jumped up from her seat, balled her fist, and—*Bam! Bam!* She nailed me on my nose. With my nose bleeding all over the floor, she shoved her index finger in my face.

"You are lucky I even let you help out with the baseball crap. You don't deserve to go anywhere else. I need you to stick around the house you creep!" Standing frozen in front of the fridge, I was afraid to move. Will she nail me again? I continued to stare at the ground, watching the puddle of blood grow.

"Now, dumbass! Go in the bathroom, and wash your nose, idiot." I staggered to the bathroom, still woozy from the shots to my face. I stuck some tissue up my nose to stop the bleeding. When I returned to the kitchen, Mom barked from her throne, "Get some paper towels and clean up your blood, Joey"

"Okay" was all I could muster. I was afraid to make eye contact with her. It may push her over the edge. I made sure to clean up the blood I could see.

I threw the towels away and went to my room, trying to figure out what I ever did to her directly or indirectly. An hour or so later, I finally built the courage to call him to give him the bad news. That was going to be a hard call for me because I was so invested in these kids. It just broke my heart. I walked back into the kitchen to call. I didn't see Mom or my brothers anywhere. With the coast clear, I called. Tommy's wife answered, "Hello, how can I help you?"

"Is coach there?"

"Hi, Joey. No, he is not here. Can I take a message?"

"Sure, can you please let him know that I can't go on the trip?"

"Oh, I am sorry to hear that. I will tell him."

"Thanks."

After 10th grade, while spending my first summer on Wigton, I enrolled into C.E.T.A. I was looking forward to not only having a job, but I would earn two credits. To me it was a no brainer. I mean I wanted to get out of the situation as soon as possible. College was not an option at this point, so I just needed to be on point, so I didn't need to stay under her roof longer than I had to.

Her drinking and abusive ways continued. She treated Greg and me like dogs but Andre and Leon could do nothing wrong in her eyes.

A week after school was out for the summer, I was assigned to work with the Rockford Housing Authority. The main office was on 15th Avenue on the other side of the river, maybe two miles away. I caught the city bus and arrived there. To my surprise, there was Betty Washington. She was a member of St. Peter's Church. She had two sons whom she was raising on her own. She walked out to the waiting area and greeted me with her big smile.

"Well, hello, Joey! Are you here on the Summer Job program?"

"Yes, ma'am," I said.

"Very good, follow me." I followed her to her office. I could not help but notice all the photos of her family. I could tell she loved her boys from past interaction with her, but she really must be proud of them to have them on display like this.

"Okay, Joey, there are three openings. There is a job here at Blackhawk Housing Projects, Orton Keyes, or Jane Addams. Do you have a preference?"

"Jane Addams," I blurted out without much thought.

"This was my old stomping ground. I still have friends there."

"Okay, then. You will report to Carl at the Center at Jane Addams at 8:00 a.m. He will give you jobs to do every day Monday through Friday. If you miss more than three days unexcused, you will not receive the two high school credits. We will pay you $3.35 per hour, which is minimum wage. Any questions?"

"No ma'am, thank you."

"Joey, please call me Betty. I will see you at church, right?"

"I plan on being there, Betty,"

"Okay then, baby, take care and tell your mama I said hello."

"Okay, will do." I didn't wait for the bus. I walked home. I was so excited to start. Who knows, maybe they will want to keep me longer than the allotted six weeks. I would be fine with being out of the house and away from Mom's wrath. She couldn't blame me if I wasn't there.

I made it home in no time. I went into the apartment to tell Mom of the plan. There she was, drunk and in a foul mood. I tried to go back outside, but she saw me. I wanted to tell her about the good news working at Jane Addams, but she probably won't want to hear it. I would just tell her tomorrow. I had time to think about it. She never gave me any love. She was quick to be irate and would often reminded me that all her woes were my fault. I could not wait for my job to begin. I loved Mom, but it was obvious that she doesn't love me. She had all of us go to counseling after we left Tyrone. I guess she realized she did real damage, but she never once took ownership for her terrible treatment of her kids. To most folks back in Dubuque, since Tyrone was out of the picture, things must be peachy. Nothing was further from the truth, and it was about to get much worse.

36
RUNNING IN PLACE

The Housing Authority had built wood cubicles in front of each apartment. My job was to stain each one so that the wood could withstand the brutal elements. It was a fun job. I got to see many of the older residents from my youth. Some of my friends were still around, too. Things were different, though. I was on a mission. I had a job to do with no time for idleness. It took a few hours to stain each cubicle. The time came when I finally reached my step-grand-mother's apartment. I had seen her over the last several days. We made small talk, but that was about it. She would be leaving her place or returning, and I would be working in the same area. I always made a point to say hi. It was not her fault things turned out so awful with Tyrone, but she knew what many people did not. June was a handful, and she needed help with her drinking problems.

This was never lost on her; in fact, before her own health took a nosedive, she would drink with the two of them. She knew things were not well with us. She was very insightful. I was always careful as far as what I would tell her. I didn't want her running to Tyrone with gossip. It was in the height of summer, and the heat was *unrelenting*. She was kind enough to make sure I had some water, and sometimes she fed me too—just like the old days

Each evening as I walked across the Morgan Street Bridge, I would just pray I would find things different at home. I wished things would change with Mom. I wish Mom could have compassion like she used to have. She just seemed all consumed with hate and malice toward me.

As the summer progressed, things continued to unravel at home. I began to consider asking Tyrone if I could live with him. I mean, I was truly afraid for my life. Desperate people do desperate things and I was at that place. Over the next few weeks I played out in my mind how I would ask him. What would I say? After all, I knew he hated me. I had nowhere else to turn here in Rockford. What was I going to do? I prayed like never before. It seemed like God was not listening because things got even worse. I finally decided I was going to ask Tyrone if I could live with him. His own sons didn't live with him. What made me think he would want anything to do with me? I must at least ask. All he can say was no.

While working at the projects, I saw him several times, coming and going from his mom's house. I didn't believe he ever saw me. If he did, he did not let on.

I continued rehearsing what I was going to say to him. After I finished staining the fence near Gail's, I decided to go to the Sandwich Factory for lunch. As I rounded a corner in the projects, there was Tyrone—in all his glory—talking to Fred a neighborhood thug.

"Joey, come here!" he bellowed. "How are you?"

"Not good," I replied as I looked right into his eyes.

"Whats going on?"

"Things are very bad. Mom is drunk all the time. She has been beating me all the time. Look, I need somewhere to live. Can I live with you?" I couldn't believe I just asked the monster if I could stay with him. He just started to laugh as he turned away from me. That was his answer? To laugh in my face? Oh, wait, this was Tyrone, after all. I should expect nothing from him. He began to once again to talk to Fred. I could see it was my queue to leave. I crossed the street and made my way back to work.

"That's fine. I can take care of myself in fact I have most of my life. Why would now be any different." I hollered at him as I crossed the street. I finished up my workday, staying clear of Gail's. His car was there, so I knew he was there. I never wanted to see or talk to him ever again.

My job ended at Jane Addams the Friday before the start of school. I was in my third year at Auburn, my focus was to take as many classes as I could. That had been my pattern since I had been in high school. As much as I would love to wrestle again this year, I couldn't. Time was flying by, and before long winter break was approaching. What I was going to do after that, I didn't know.

Christmas came and went. I had come to hate the holidays. To me it meant I must be around her instead of in school. I would rather have the meanest, nastiest teacher at school than to deal with her. Tyrone had Leon and Andre at his house for Christmas break. Marty and Greg were staying with Mark, and Toots worked all the time. That just left me at home with her. I spent all my idle time in my room.

37
BIG PLANS

During my time in high school I had known kids who joined the military. I had no desire to go to college. I began to ponder the idea of joining the military. I knew I must come up with a plan and soon. Monday morning, as I made my way into the school, I noticed a bunch of recruiters talking to some students near the entrance. I instantly made my way over to the men in uniform. I worked my way to the front of the crowd just as the Navy recruiter began to share the history of the naval service. I was hooked! After his two-minute spiel, he said "All of us recruiters will be in the counselors' offices all day. If you want to learn more about the military or if you have questions, come see us." He didn't have to tell me twice!

I spent my entire lunch period talking to the Army, Navy, Marines, and Air Force representatives. I bounced from one table to another. I grabbed all the brochures I could carry. With lunch period winding down, I saw my chance to once again make small talk with recruiters. All the other students were long gone, and it seemed like I was the center of their attention. After I asked more questions of the other three branches, I really felt drawn to the Navy's table. My grandpa was in the Navy. With just five minutes left of lunch period, I hustled back to the table. There the Navy guy was shifting through a huge pile of questionnaires. He looked up from the pile, smiled, and said, "Hello, young man. My name is

Andy." He had graying thin brown hair with a flip over. His face was aged with what appeared to be the results of years of smoking. Andy reached out to shake my hand. He had a dark olive color skin and dark brown eyes. I could see in his eyes something I did not see with the other recruiters. He asked me about myself, my interests, and my hobbies. Maybe this was just a ploy, but for anyone to take interest in me got my attention.

"Really quickly, son, let me tell you about what we can do for you. With that, Andy proceeded to tell me about the Navy's various programs and opportunities. I didn't want to seem eager, but that just seemed like something right up my alley. I needed to come up with a plan soon. Maybe just maybe the service was the way to go. Just as if on cue, the bell rang indicating lunch was over. As I gathered my things I said, "Thanks for your time, sir. I will be in touch."

"Sounds good, son. Have a good day!" I exited into the hallway daydreaming about life in the Navy. I thought it would make my grandpa so proud.

When I arrived home, I saw Mom and the boys in the living room watching TV. As I walked through the living room, Mom gave me a look. I knew that look, it was an 'I hate you' look. She didn't say a word. She didn't need to. I knew where I stood in her eyes. I was the gunk on the bottom of her shoe. That's fine! I said hi to the four boys as I passed through and into my room. The thought began to run through my mind *I just might have my ticket out from under her roof once and for all.*

I got my homework done in no time flat. I cold focus all my attention on the military packets I brought home. I could hear everyone in the kitchen. It must be dinnertime. I didn't care. I was not hungry. I was so engrossed in the material until I fell asleep.

37
DREAMING BIG

Over the next several weeks, I memorized all I could about all four branches. They all seemed to have good qualities, but the Navy seemed to appeal to me the most. I decided to stop by the Navy office downtown at the Federal Building. I found the office with Andy behind his desk, smoking a cigarette.

"Can I help you?" he asked "Sure, I want to learn more about the Navy."

"Okay, sure. Sit down here, and I would like to get some basic information from you if I could."

"I gave you all of my info at Auburn, sir."

"What is your name again?"

"Joey Potosi."

"Oh, Yes! Your grandpa was in World War II, right?" he asked.

"Yes, he was, sir."

"Hey, Joey, don't call me sir. I work for a living." I wanted to tell him to brush off his shirt. He had ashes from the cigarette all over his uniform jacket.

"Take a seat. I need to pull your info, son." He turned his back to me rifling through a stack of papers behind his desk.

"Okay, here we are," he said as he continued to hot box his cancer stick. I was trying to hide the fact that I was so excited about this whole Navy thing. I just wanted to see what the catch was. Everything had a catch. I guess time will tell.

"Okay, son, if you are serious about the Navy, you will need to take a series of tests. I am going to send some forms home with you. Since you are a minor, you will need to have your folks sign this paperwork."

"Well, my Mom is the only one. Dad is not around."

"Oh, sorry, son. Where is he?"

"I don't know. He left years ago."

"Okay that's not a problem. I need you to be up front with me about one thing, kid."

"What is that?"

"Do you have a criminal record?"

"No."

"Okay, because we do have to run a background check on you. If it turns out that you are lying, and you have a record, you can't join my Navy, not to mention you would be wasting my time. I don't like kids to lie to me!"

"No, Andy, I don't have a record"

"Very well, then. Here you go." He stood up as he handed me a folder full of forms Mom will have to fill out.

Oh boy, I thought as I exited the building and began the long walk home. The bus station was nearby, but the buses stopped running an hour ago. So I started the trip home when the thought crossed my mind. *Will the fact that I ran away disqualify me? Oh, my God!* I began to cry as I replayed in my mind what Andy said.

"If you have a record and you don't disclose that information voluntarily, you will be disqualified." *Do I really have a record? I was put in jail because I ran away does that count?* I was racking my brain over this. I hoped not.

I was walking over the bridge when I heard a car honk at me as it passed me on the road. It was Andy! "Where you headed, Joey?"

"On the south side, on Wigton." I watched as Andy pulled over, motioning for me to get in. I ran as fast as I could to his little black Omni.

"Thanks, Andy. What a cool car!"

"Thanks! Joey, it's too cold for you to be walking in this crap. Does your mom have a car? Why didn't you call her for a ride?"

"We don't have a car, and besides I don't think she cares that I have to walk."

"I see. So, tell me where to go." I gave him directions to the house. The idea of having a record was killing me.

"Andy, I have a confession. I ran away from home. My stepdad took me to juvenile the following day, I guess to be hateful. So, I don't know if that means I have a record."

"Thanks for sharing that little bit of information. Tell me this. Were you arrested from your home? Or were you put on any kind of probation?"

"No, sir, oops. I mean no, Andy"

"Well in that case it sounds like you are fine. Is there anything else, anything at all?"

"Nope that's it!"

"Okay, then, that's good." As we pulled up in front of the house, I thought Andy could tell that I was nervous about asking Mom to sign all this paperwork. As I thanked him for the ride and excused myself, Andy asked," Hey, is your Mom home? If she is, I will be glad to explain everything to her."

"Would you really? I am sure she is home." I looked on as Andy exited the little Omni and trudged through the snow on the ushoveled driveway.

I led Andy into the front door. From there I could see Mom sitting at the kitchen table smoking a cigarette. As I entered the kitchen with Andy, I said, "Hey Mom, how are you?"

Without even looking at me, she barked, "I am peachy, creep! Who is this?"

"My name is Andy, ma'am. I am the Navy recruiter. Joey met me at the school several weeks ago. He paid me a visit downtown today, expressing his interest in joining the Navy.

"I see. So, what does it have to do with me?"

"Well ma'am. I am sorry, what is your name?"

"My name is June." I pulled out a chair for Andy to sit down. I thought to myself, *Mom can you be any more rude? At least offer the man a seat. I mean he was taking his time to talk to you!* Once seated, Andy began to explain in detail the Navy and all it offered.

I looked on as he went through the same spiel that he shared with me at school.

"Well," Mom finally spoke up. "I will sign all the paperwork you have. I want him out of here as soon as possible. But I know he will never make it!" she said emphatically. I did not say a word. I wanted her to focus on signing her name on all the forms Andy gave her.

After she signed the last form, she turned to me with the cold, hateful look.

"Let me tell you something, loser!" Her whole demeanor changed. She turned in her seat to face me. With her left index finger an inch from my face and her other hand balled up in a fist, she ripped into me.

"When you get kicked out of the service, you can't come back here to live! Maybe you can live in the Rescue Mission with your father!" I sat there in utter embarrassment. All I could do was stare at the ground. It was taking all my willpower to hold back the tears. She paused her rant long enough to light up a cancer stick. Andy spoke up just as she repositioned herself to get even closer to me. It was almost like he was not even there.

"Well, it looks like all of the papers are in order, June. Once everything is processed, including the background check, we can proceed." He stoodup to shake her hand. She shook his hand with her all-too-famous fake smile.

"Thanks for your time. Have a good one," she said as she walked him to the front door. That was my chance to go to bed. I just hoped she didn't come back to my room. I ran into my room and jumped under the blankets. I didn't even bother to undress. I laid on my back, covering my head with the blankets, dreading what was in store. I could see into the kitchen. I was just waiting for her arrival.

To my surprise, I saw the kitchen go black, and I could hear her walk to her room. Thank God! I could go to sleep in peace. I tossed and turned, unable to sleep. All I kept thinking about was Dad. Was he in the mission in Dubuque? Was he here in Rockford? I finally drifted off to sleep, hoping to see him soon.

The next morning I caught the smell of instant coffee. Mom loved her coffee I wanted to ask her about Dad's whereabouts. I hoped she was in a good mood. As I walked into the kitchen, I saw all the boys sitting around the table eating cereal.

"Hey, Joey," the boys said in unison.

"Hi, guys," I responded. As I went to pour a bowl of cereal, Greg blurted out," No more milk, man."

"Why didn't you save me some milk?"

"Joey, mix up some powdered milk," Mom hollered. I looked back to where she was sitting at the table. She was writing a letter to someone.

"Can I go to Eagles to buy some milk? I hate powdered milk."

"I don't have any food stamps. Deal with it."

"Okay who are you writing to?" I asked.

"I am writing to Lynn, why? Is it any of your business?" I turned back to the counter and poured the cereal back into the box. I skipped breakfast and went into my room. I pulled out all the brochures about the Navy. I had read them so many times, I had practically memorized the contents. I wished Dad would come around. I wanted to tell him about my decision to join the military. Maybe I would get that chance. All I could do was hope.

39
A NEW POSITION

The second semester of eleventh grade was well underway. The deadline came and went for the coaches to register and begin to compile the teams. Although I had plans to coach again this spring at the center, Mom needed me at home when she picked up odd jobs. The odd jobs she could find didn't last long. Within a few weeks, she was home every evening. It was too late for me to join the team at the Center. I just needed to focus on my studies.

I got home from school on Monday, and I didn't see Mom anywhere. This was not odd as Mom was usually upstairs, drinking with Peggy. Toots was in the kitchen preparing dinner when a call came in.

"Hello," Toots said into the phone.

"Joey, it is for you," she said. Who could it be, oh maybe Andy.

"Yes, can I help you? "Hi Joey, this is Stan Johnson from Northwest Community Center. We are looking for umpires for the season. We are wondering if you are interested. I know you have a history here of coaching, so it may be a good fit for you. We pay thirty dollars per game. What do you think?" Without a once of hesitation, I replied, "Yes, I would love to."

I walked up to Northwest after school the next day. I had a brief meeting with Stan. He gave me a quick rundown of what my job would entail. After the meeting, Stan stood up and walked me to the main entrance. As we got to the front door, he handed me a thick book.

"Thank you for joining the team. Here is the rulebook. This is your Bible. Study it frontwards and backwards. The season starts next week. I need you to be ready."

"You can count on me, sir," I said as I shook his hand. I spent whatever free time I had during the week memorizing all the rules.

Game Day

Monday was here. My first game would start soon. I completed my homework during study hall. As I began the short walk to the Center, I started to feel nervous about my first game. I arrived at Stan's office. Stan greeted me with a big smile.

"Hello, Joey, here are the items you are here for. I have assigned you to field two. Good luck! By the way, we need more umpires. If you know of anyone who may be interested, have them call me."

"Okay, will do," I said as I gathered the items and walked out.

It was tough going that first game. Yeah, I earned $30 bucks, but I ran my butt off. I was the only ump covering the game. I had to make all the calls on the field. I recorded the score of the game, and so forth, and I went into Stan's office to let him know how it went.

"So, Joey, how did it go? I walked up to the game you were umping, and I was impressed with your effort. Thank you." Wow, I was on cloud nine with the accolades.

"Well, Stan, I thank you for the chance, but I need help umping the games."

"Do you have any friends that may want to help out? If so, bring them to the next game you will be umping, and we will give them a chance. If they work out, I will pay you extra."

"Okay. I will ask at school." Maybe my friend Vern would like to do it

At school on Friday, I asked my friend Vern if he would like to make some money. He agreed. I gave him a rulebook and informed him on when and where to be.

Game day was here and no Vern. Here I was once again running my butt off. It was very difficult umping a game by myself. I just wished I could get some help. At the top of the third inning, Vern arrived. I was ticked about him not being on time but grateful he was here now. After the game, Vern helped me to return the bases and score sheet. We got paid, and that was a good feeling.

My reasoning behind the whole umping thing was to stay out of Mom's hair, not to mention interacting with the kids. It seemed like she was at my throat more and more while I was at home. I didn't understand it at all, but at least I had this outlet. Stan gave me the game schedule for next week's series of games. To my fright, I saw that I was assigned to the White Sox game. I was guessing many of these kids were the same ones I coached last year. I had seen many of them in passing at the Center. Several have asked why I was not coaching this year. I really didn't have a good answer for them. I wished I was coaching them, but now I was committed to umping. I agreed to that, so that was what I would do.

The dreadful day came when I had to umpire the White Sox game. They were facing the Orioles. I thought that was ironic. When I played at Northwest, I played on the Oriole team. That was a long time ago, and they had all new coaches, but secretly I was routing for my team, the White Sox.

All the coaches met with me before the game to hand over the line-ups, and so on. It was a quick visit. I was happy to see Tommy. He was still a friend. He taught me a lot about the inner workings of the game. I had a lot of respect for that man. After our little visit, I called the game into play. Vern was there; I put him on first base, and I took home plate. It quickly was turning into an exciting game—a little too exciting for one parent.

This random father didn't like the calls I was making behind the plate. I stopped the game to ask him to settle down. He was cursing like a drunken sailor. With all these kids here, I was not going to allow this guy who appeared drunk to continue his act. I decided the next time he had a fit, I would eject him from the game. The rulebook stated I had the authority to eject unruly parents. I had never been in this situation, but here I was now dealing with this jerk. We were all here for the kids. It was an experience they will have all their lives. I was not going to let him ruin it for anyone. Of course, it would affect his child in some way, but for the better good of the center. I was determined to make a move. Besides, being around a drunk for most of my life was something I hated with a passion. I wanted everyone to have a good time. Not five minutes later, I called one of the kids from the Orioles out on strikes. The father was furious. He started up on me again. Tommy, the coach from the White Sox, asked him to settle down before he would be asked to leave. He was enraged.

"Hey, ump! What are you calling? That last pitch was a ball. It was on the outside!" he screamed at the top of his lungs. I knew it would do no good to argue with the man. I was sweating profusely in the heat—not to mention the stress of how to deal with him.

I had no choice but to halt the game once again. I looked over to Vern and waved him over for some support. I looked on as he ran to home plate.

"What's up, man?"

"I am going to eject this guy. I need you to back me up!"

"No problem!" We both walked over to the drunken dad.

"Sir, I need you to leave the ballpark."

"Screw you! I ain't going anywhere!"

"That's fine," I said. The game will not resume until you leave." I turned around and walked back over to home plate. He was sitting behind the third base dugout. I could see Tommy go over to him. I couldn't hear what was being said. Whatever it was, the dad decided to leave. That was a relief.

"Okay. Play ball." The White Sox went on to win the game. I could not be happier for Tommy and his team

When I got home, I was dropped back into reality. Mom was in her bedroom, sitting on her bed drinking a beer, and inhaling her cancer stick. She was smashed as usual. I was hoping the boys were already in bed. I poked my head into the their bedrooms. They were sound asleep. Thank God.

I wanted to tell Mom that I went through with joining the Navy. I walked to her room. She looked up at me as I stood in the doorway.

"What do you need, Joey?"

"I passed all the tests; I am in the Navy now."

"Oh well you will never make it! You are a piece of crap just like your dad!" I just turned around and went to bed. All I thought about was that glorious day when I will leave here, never to return.

40
CHANGE OF ADDRESS

Sunday morning was like any other Sunday. Toots and I got the kids fed and dressed for church. The church van picked us on time for Sunday school. With the service finally over, my brothers and I raced to the church van. When we pulled into the driveway, there was Dad sitting on the porch. I forced my way past Toots who was still sitting in her seat. I ran as fast as I could toward Dad. He had a huge smile on his face as he stood up and ran toward me.

"Hey, Joey! How are you?"

"I am better now!" After his embrace, I looked on as he hugged Toots, Marty, and Greg. When he turned back toward me, I noticed he was crying.

'Why are you crying, Terry? Do you feel guilty? You should; you are a joke!" Mom screamed as she exited the van.

"Hi, June. You look good."

"You don't! You look hung over. Have you been drinking?"

"No, I have not. I have been working a lot for the temp service. I have something for you. Dad handed Mom a wad of money.

"It's about time, loser!" Dad redirected his attention to us kids. Toots introduced him to Andre and Leon. This was the first time he had met my two younger brothers. He looked awkward as he greeted them with a handshake. They didn't know who he was. I had told them about my dad. So did Mom. In fact, she had bad-mouthed him for years.

"Okay, you guys stay out here. Terry, come with me," she said as she led him into the house.

After about ten minutes I looked through the front room window. I could see they were sitting at the kitchen table drinking coffee. Mom was talking to Dad about something. I couldn't really make it out. She must have heard me on the porch. She turned around and marched to the front door.

"Where are the other kids?"

"I don't know."

"Go find them; we are going to have a meeting." I bolted off the porch and ran around the front of the house. I didn't have to look far. They were sitting on the stairs, leading up to Peggy's apartment. Peggy was sitting with them, smoking a joint.

"Hey guys, Mom wants us in the house."

"For what man?" Greg asked.

"I don't know, but there is something big going on, I think." Leon and Andre ran as fast as they could, beating the rest of us back into the house. I saw that Mom and Dad were now sitting in the living room as I entered.

"Okay," Mom said.

"It looks like everyone is here. I have some news for you all."

She was pacing back and forth, inhaling her cancer stick. I could see she was nervous about something. She continued to pace without saying a word staring at the ground. She finally said, "I have struggled to find work and real contentment here. I have decided to move us back to Dubuque. I put down a small deposit on an apartment. I looked at the last time I was in Dubuque." *Wow*, I thought. *What does this all mean*? I was planning on finishing up at Auburn, so I could graduate after first semester. Was that going to mess up my plans?' It was so quiet in the room. I didn't know what the others were thinking, but I was concerned about my future.

"Wait Mom, will this affect my finishing school? I have been sworn into the Navy. I am obligated now."

"Joey, Joey! I am sure Senior or Hempstead will accept your credits!" she snapped at me.

"Okay, I hope so. I want to join the Navy really bad."

"Is Dad moving in with us?" Marty asked. I looked at Toots as she rolled her eyes at that idea.

"No, he is not. He has a lot to prove to me before I would ever even consider that! He is going to help us move, though.

"Everything will be fine, Joey. Don't worry," he said. I studied his face for a long time. He was the one who was going to rescue us from Tyrone or so I thought. Every day I would hope he would just show up and set all of us free.

I wanted to scream from the top of my lungs, "Dad, where have you been? Do you have any idea what we all have been through?" That would be pointless. Toots will be leaving for college tomorrow. In a few short months, I would be gone as well. I was glad he was here. He needed to get back into Mom's good graces. Maybe, just maybe, he could be a father to Marty and Greg. Tyrone was the only father they really knew. That was not saying much!

"I need you guys to start packing your clothes. I have boxes out front. Toots, go help Leon and Andre. I will help Marty and Greg."

"June, I need to get back to the Mission. Check in is at 3:00 p.m."

"Okay, Terry. I need you here next Saturday. Don't be late. Brian will be here with the U-Haul."

"Okay," he replied as he walked out the front door. He didn't even say goodbye. Will we see him again? I hoped so

Dubuque, Here We Come.

Everything became a blur, and Saturday, moving day, was now upon us. Ma had hired Brian, my cousin Lisa's husband and one of his friends to move us. Since the boys would not be much help now, and Toots has moved away to college, she decided that all four of them should go to Dubuque ahead of us. So, it was me, my dad, who was back in our lives on a very limited basis, Brian, his friend Hank, and Mom.

It took a long time to load up the U-Haul. It was so hot and miserable. Finally done, we all went to the truck when we realized we could not all sit in the cab. As it turned out, Mom expected me and my dad to ride in the back of the U-Haul with our belongings like dogs. I was used to being treated like a dog, but now I must travel two-plus hours in the back of a U-Haul. Dad objected.

"Hey, one of you adults should sit in the back and let Joey sit up front." I was so glad he spoke up, but Mom quickly shut him up." 'Get you and your son in the back, and shut the hell up!' He didn't say another word. He climbed in the truck with me and found a spot on the floor to sit.

As Brian closed the door, he said," Don't worry, we will stop plenty of times to let you guys stretch and get some fresh air." With that, down came the door. Now we were in utter darkness.

"Gee, what a nice guy, huh, Dad?"

"Yeah, well, he will make stops for us.

Surprisingly, during the trip, Dad asked a lot of questions. He wanted to know more about Toots, Marty, and Greg. In the back of my mind, I was thinking, *Great, now Dad is back and I am leaving. How is that right? I hope he stays off the booze!* "Joey, why did you enlist in the Navy and not the Army?" I never thought he would ask.

"Well, besides the fact that Grandpa was in the Navy, I think it will be a better fit for me."

"I know you will be successful. I also know you are mad at me for not being in your life. I am sorry! I want to make it up to you."

"The biggest way you can make it up to me is—" Before I could tell him, I felt the truck come to a halt. The back door flung open.

"Hey guys. Are you doing okay?" Brian asked with a glazed look in his eyes.

"We are perfect," Dad blurted out as he got to his feet and exited the truck. I followed him eager to get some fresh air. Once I got my bearings, I recognized where we were—the gas station in Stockton. This was the halfway point to Dubuque. We as a family had made countless stops here, going to and from Dubuque.

As I walked by the cab of the truck, I could smell the stench of weed. Yep, Ma and the boys were getting high. As I walked to the restroom, I saw her staggering as she made her way back to the truck.

"Mom, what happened to letting us out to get fresh air? Did you forget we were back there?"

"Uh, no, Joey, we just want to get to Dubuque." Wow, disregard the safety of your kid to get what she wants once again.

I turned around and make a beeline to the bathroom. I took my time getting back to the truck. As I walked by the passenger side of the U-Haul, Mom said.

"It's about time! "I could see Dad and Brian talking at the back of the truck.

"Are you ready, Joey?"

"Yeah, I guess."

Once in the truck, Brian closed the door, and off we went. I wanted to ask Dad so many things. A short time later, I heard him snoring away. I wasn't letting him off the hook. I need some answers to some questions. The number one thing I wanted to ask was why. I made my way over to where he was sleeping. I shook him awake.

"Dad, when I saw you at Grandma's, you promised you would get involved in our lives. Why haven't you?" He sat up and scratched his head.

"I wanted to, but things happened" he said unconvincingly." What things? Booze or what? You have four children that have needed you. For years now, I had hoped every day you would show up and fix everything. You were my hero. I say 'were' because you are nothing more than a homeless, helpless drunk! I hope for your sake and for my brothers, you can get your act together!" I was standing over Dad, waiting for a response. He laid down once again without saying a word. I didn't think he knew what to say.

After some time, I could feel the truck coming to a complete stop. The door flew open. The racket woke up Dad then we both exited the truck.

"We are here, boys," Mom said." She was standing at the back of the truck, smoking her beloved cigarette. She led us to the apartment. It was a yellow apartment building that sat on the corner of 13th and Elm. We took a quick walk through and then got to the business at hand. Mom seemed like she had sobered off the weed. She was very excited about being here, obviously. I was just hoping she starts to treat me better. It could be that now that she was near her family, she would. With the five of us unloading the U-Haul, it went very quickly.

Once we were settled in, we said goodbye to Brian and his friend. "Well, I am going to go to Lynn's. Terry, do you want to go?"

"No, I need to check in at the Mission."

"Dad, go with us" I said. "The boys will be here later."

"No! Go to the Mission, Terry. Thanks for your help," Mom barked. I looked on as Dad walked away with his head down. Mom and I walked over to my Aunt Lynn's house. She was one of Mom's older sisters and one of my favorite people in the whole world. She had not boasted about how she had helped us in the past like others. In fact, she had been a huge help in many ways. Her only son Vince and I were close. He was a good kid, just misdirected like the rest of us. There were four girls in the family as well. We all got along. They, like us, were the black sheep of the family.

Once we arrived, Mom walked through the back yard to the back door. I stopped to say "hi" to Vince. He gave me a huge hug. 'Hey man! I am glad you are here!' "Me, too. Are the boys here?"

"No, but Mom, Dad and the girls are in the kitchen" he said. I walked through the back door. As I entered the kitchen, I said, "I have missed you guys so much!"

"We missed you, too, Joey," Lynn said as she pulled me into her large frame.

"I love you, Lynn." Little did I know that going to Lynn's house would become a regular occurrence. I just loved my time there. Her family was dirt poor just like us, but she could stretch out a dollar bill like no one's business. Within moments, we were sitting around the table sharing fun memories when I asked, "Where are the boys, Lynn?"

"Jane is bringing them here in an hour," she said with a big smile on her face.

"Good," I replied. I won't really relax until I was reunited with them.

I was sitting at the kitchen table with everyone making small talk until I saw Marty come flying into the kitchen. He ran right up to me.

"I am glad you guys are here, Joey."

"I am, too, man! Greg, Leon, and Andre soon made their way into the house. I was so happy to see my brothers. It had only been a few days since I last saw them. They were a sight for sore eyes. Greg walked over to me and asked, "How is the apartment, Joey?"

"It's a lot nicer than Wigton."

"Do I get my own room?"

"I don't know, man, ask Mom," I said. Marty and the other boys overheard Greg's question and looked in my direction as if I had any say so.

"Greg, you will have a bedroom! Don't worry about it. As of now, Joey will be in the basement." I guess they were content with that answer. All I keep thinking was, "Finally a new beginning. Will it be a fresh start with me and Mom? Will Dad try to be in our lives, or will he stay away? I couldn't help to think about what the next day, weeks, and months will bring. Time will tell. It was getting late. I hoped we could get home soon. I was dead tired. Mom must be, too. Just then Mom said, "So, Lynn, we are going to head home" as she stood up from the kitchen table.

"Rick, give these guys a ride home. It's been a long day for June and Joey."

"Okay, let's go," he said. Rick never said much of anything. I guess that was why I liked him. When he did say anything, it was usually funny.

As we all headed out to the station wagon, I said, "Hey, Mom I want to walk to the apartment."

"Okay. Who wants to go with him?"

"I do," Marty said.

"Alright, you guys walk straight to the apartment."

"We will," I said.

Marty and I began the short walk home. I could tell he was studying the new neighborhood. As we zig and zag our way to the apartment, Marty said, "It looks a lot different than Rockford."

"Yes, it is!" I remarked.

Mom and the boys were already in the apartment laying down on the floor of the living room when we entered through the front door.

"Grab a blanket and pillow and find a spot to sleep. Marty and I quickly grabbed a blanket and pillow and found a place to sleep. I couldn't sleep. All I could focus on was the fact that in just a matter of days, school will be starting, and the countdown into the Navy will begin.

41
TICK TOCK; THE COUNTDOWN BEGINS

I t took a good part of the day to get completely settled into our new place. I got the bedroom in the basement. The limestone was dirty and musty-smelling, but I would make it work. Half of the basement floor was concrete. The other half of my room floor was dirt. I was not sure why the landlord never finished it. One good thing was I didn't see any roaches anywhere. The last apartment was crawling with them. Mom insisted we keep a clean place. No matter how clean the place was, we could never rid ourselves of the pests.

On Sunday, with all the heavy work now done, Mom allowed us to play outside. We were now living in the area known as "The Flats." Dubuque had many hills and bluffs. This area, however, was flat. In fact, before the floodwall was installed in the 1960s, this area would flood twice a year. Most of the other areas of town were spared. That was because many of the other neighborhoods sat on a hill. Thus, many of the residents who lived in "The Flats" did so out of necessity, not choice. In fact, as I would find out over time, the clear majority of the folks in our new neighborhood were poor.

Soon we discovered train tracks behind the apartment. The tracks were a block behind the house so it was hard to resist running to the tracks when we heard the whistle blow as the train traveled thru the area several times a day. Greg had a bright idea to jump on the slow moving train as it passed directly behind the apartment.

"Greg! What are you doing? That's a good way to get killed"! I screamed. Greg hopped on the train and waved for us to join him. There was no way I was doing that. As I turned away and walked to the front of the house I could no longer see Marty, Leon or Vince. I was looking high and low for the boys but I couldn't find them. I walked back to the tracks and what I saw next caused my heart to sink! There was Marty, Leon and Vince climbing onto the moving train.

"You guys jump off!" I screamed. They looked back at me laughing hysterically. I walked into the back yard hoping and praying they will be ok as I watched the train roll out of sight. A short time later I could see the boys walking along the tracks toward the apartment. It looked like they were ok. I had always been afraid of trains. My uncle Hank had lost his leg to a train. As a very young child he fell asleep on the tracks. Unfortunately a train came a long and cut his leg clean off. He was fortunate to have survived. Ever since I heard that story I have had a profound respect for trains. There was no way i was going to go train jumping.

42
BIG PROJECT

M onday was here and so was the start of school. Apparently, Mom enrolled the boys in the schools in the neighborhood earlier in the summer. However, she received a letter from the Dubuque School District concerning my status.

The Board of Education in Dubuque would not accept many of my previous credits. All that meant was that I would have to go to school for the entire year. I was devastated. I had already sworn into the Navy. Upon further research, my Mom discovered that I could go to Central High School. Central took kids who were either kicked out of other high schools or were just high risk youth. I really didn't want to go there but I didn't have a choice. I also knew ma wanted me gone as soon as possible. She reminded me daily of this fact."

Tuesday afternoon

My cousin Jenny drove me and Mom over to the school to get registered. When we arrived there, I saw a bunch of people playing hacky sack in the back of the school. I walked back there to see if I recognized anyone from the last time I lived here. Right off the bat, I saw Bruce. *Holy crap!* I thought. *This jerk goes here?* We got into a fistfight during my last stay in Dubuque. To be honest, back then he intimidated me. We were the same size but he had a real crazy side to him. But if he wanted to get jumpy with me, I was more than willing to beat him senseless if need be. I was just hoping I was not going to be stuck in the same class as him.

After I got registered I was given my schedule. I only needed two credits.

My first class was English with a teacher named George. One of the cool rules here at Central was that the teachers were called by their first name. That was very different. He was a tall man with a bushy beard and long brown hair. He had a strong New York accent. I thought he was really cool. He was so laid back on my first day. He seemed very popular with the other students.

The bell rang, indicating the class was over. I thought the first period went very well. After writing down the homework assignment, I gathered my items and made my way upstairs. Sociology with John was my second and last class of the day. As I entered the room, I didn't see anyone. Just as I picked out a desk, I heard a booming voice from behind me.

"Hello, young man. What is your name?" I turned to see who just spoke. There stood a very large man. He was six feet, five inches, and 300 pounds. He had black hair, beard, and wire rim glasses. He stared at me, waiting for a response, I spoke up.

"My name is Joey Potosi, sir." He looked down at a list of names on a spiral notebook.

"I didn't see your name," he replied. I began to panic.

"I just registered today. He continued to feverishly scan over the list, looking for my name.

"You will need to report to the office. I'm sure it is a simple oversight." He turned away from me and greeted the other students as they walked into the classroom. I could see he was checking off the names of each student. I grabbed my book bag, all the while thinking, *What does this mean*? Just as I began the descent down the stairs, he barged out of his room and approached the stairwell.

"Joey, I called the office. They forgot to tell me you would be added to my class. Come back up." I exhaled a sigh of relief. What a relief. I didn't need any setbacks. As I once again entered the classroom.

"Welcome to Sociology. And please don't call me sir. My name is John."

"Okay," I managed to say. As it turned out, he began the class by giving the history of Vietnam. He proceeded to tell the class that we as a group will be publishing a book on the topic. He was giving us the whole semester to accomplish this. It was going to be a huge assignment. Each of us was given a list of local veterans. There was a list of ten questions. He instructed us that we can interview them in person or via phone.

I was nervous about this. I didn't know a thing about Vietnam. I was very curious to speak with these men, though. As I prepared to go into the military in just a few months, maybe I could glean something from these vets. Bruce was not in either of the classes I was in. The bell rang, and I was so relieved. I was worried that the classes would be very tough. When I last lived here, I struggled mightily. That thought was very fresh in my mind. Over the next several weeks, I conducted the twelve interviews via the telephone, as I did not have a way to meet the guys in person. Besides, I was too insecure to meet these war heroes in person. The questions I had to ask were very personal in nature. However, I learned a ton about Vietnam.

Over the next couple of months, that project became my baby. Along with others in the school, the hope was to compile our findings and publish a book to educate the public. It took some time, but when October rolled around, the book was completed and in my hands. I was so proud of that accomplishment. As a future military person, I learned so much from these people. I will never forget them. This book was one of my greatest achievements up to this point.

I excelled at Central. I was on the Dean's list. That was a first for me. I was doing everything to the fullest so that I could leave as planned. It was not lost on me as well that Mom wanted the same.

42
GYM RATS

At some point, Mom got us all memberships at the YMCA. They were offering free memberships to those who qualified. We were poorer than dirt. I guess that qualified us. On that first weekend, Lynn came by to pick us up bright and early." Where are the girls?" Greg asked as he climbed into the back next to Vince.

"They are girls, Greg! They are too lazy," Vince replied through his laughter. Once all loaded up in her rusty station wagon, we took off. Leon and Andre were excited. They loved to play in the pool. I could tell Marty was excited, too. He had taken up break dancing. He was good at it. He had made a bunch of friends in the neighborhood. They all hung out at Jackson Park most nights, refining their skills. Up to this point, I had not taken much interest in break dancing. I liked to go and hang out with Marty. I tried to support him as much as possible. He was so talented and strong. I really didn't know how he could dance like that, especially when he spun on his head. It gave me a headache just watching him. They were a bunch of good kids. In fact, all my brothers liked to hang out with the same group of kids. At least when I leave for the Navy, I thought they would be surrounded with a good core.

She pulled into the parking lot at the YMCA, puffing the life out of her cigarette as if it was the last one she would smoke. We started to exit the car when Lynn said," I will be here in three hours. Please be out front, so I don't have to track you all down."

"Okay," we all responded in unison.

"Leon and Andre were going swimming. What are you guys going to do?"

"Vince and I are going to lift weights, man," Greg said as he and Vince walk past me.

"Marty, are you swimming with us?"

"Some of my friends from Jackson Park may be here. They practice the newest dance moves in the gym. If they are here I will just work out with them."

"Alright, you guys, just please be here outside in three hours, okay?" Greg looked back at me and nodded his head.

Leon, Andre, and I made our way to the locker room to change into our trunks. Within five minutes, we were playing in the pool. We had such a great time, just the three of us. I really wanted to lift weights, but I was glad I decided to do this instead. The water felt so good. It had been so hot and muggy. Leon had struggled adjusting to the new town, not to mention being so far from his dad. Andre seemed like he was adjusting well. He was a free spirit, laid back like Toots.

I began to wonder if the others were going to join us. Just then they all came running out of the locker room. To see the excitement on their faces was priceless. The next time I looked up at the clock, it was time to go. *Oh crap!* I thought. Everyone was at the other end of pool, goofing around. I hollered, "Hey, we have to go! Lynn will be here in fifteen minutes to pick us up." I looked on as they exited the pool and went into the locker room to get changed. We all got showered and changed in no time flat. As we walked out front, I informed the boys.

"If we abide by Lynn's demands, I bet she will bring us up here every weekend if we ask her."

"That would be awesome," Andre said with a big smile on his face.

"What do you think, Vince? Will she?"

"Maybe; it depends on what she has going on."

"Okay cool."

"Greg did you get a good workout?"

"I sure did, Joey. It was a lot of fun"

Lynn pulled up right on time. There she was with a big smile on her face.

"How was the Y, boys?"

"It was awesome, Mom," Vince said.

"Do you think we can come up every Saturday?"

"I don't see why not as long as you all are getting something out of it."

"Wow, thanks, Lynn," Leon said.

"No problem. I love you boys. I want to see you happy.

True to her word over the next several weeks without fail, Lynn took us to the YMCA. It was always the same routine. Marty, Greg, and Vince went off to do their thing. I was content taking Leon and Andre swimming. I so loved spending time with them.

43
A PROMISE KEPT

Since I was out of school by 10:30 a.m. I wanted to find other things to do with my time. I enjoyed running for exercise, but I also liked to lift weights. Up until this point, I had not had a chance to lift, I wanted to change that. The YMCA was up the street about a mile on Dodge. I decided on Monday to walk up there after school. I needed to do all I could to be ready for boot camp.

While working out, an older gentleman offered to spot me as I bench-pressed. I had seen him in the pool before. He was very fit for his age. Over the many visits to the YMCA, we developed a friendship. One day while working out he asked, "Do you live by St. Mary's?"

"Yes, I do. Why do you ask?"

"I am Father Troy, the priest at the parish. I have seen you walking around in the area."

"We live on 13th and Elm." After our brief exchange, he left to the locker room, and I continued to work out. Soon we would cross paths again. In fact, the very next week, we became workout partners, and he became my ride home.

I felt I had a spiritual component as a child. I was not Catholic, but I was curious as to what the church taught. My grandparents had reminded me many times they wanted me to receive my communion and confirmation before entering the Navy. I swore to them, I would fulfill that wish one day. I wanted to do it for them. Maybe this was the time to do it. I decided to talk to Father Troy during our workout.

Saint Columbkille's was the only Catholic church I was remotely familiar with. I would go there with Grandma and on a rare occasion with Grandpa over the years during my summer visits. The Mass was in a strange language, which I discovered later was Latin. I never understood a word spoken, but I didn't think it mattered. I really thought most the people didn't have a clue, either.

With Monday here, and my weekly workout with Fr Troy at the YMCA, I needed to ask him about helping me. After our workout, while driving home, I built up the courage.

"I am wondering how much it costs for catechism classes? I want to go through the process before I go into the Navy."

"Well," Fr Troy said, "As a matter of fact, I am going to offer the classes to you for free if you are interested.

"You will do that for me? Thank you so very much. When can I start?"

"Let me look at the calendar, and I will tell you later in the week. We will meet one-on-one since the official class has already began."

"Awesome!" I was so excited about his kind gesture that I didn't even notice we were sitting in front of the apartment.

"Thanks again," I blurted out as I ran into the apartment. I usually waved goodbye as Fr Troy would pull off. Not today. I was so excited, I ran right by my mom and down into my bedroom. I spent my entire free time down there over the next few days after school and the YMCA, just absorbing all the material Fr Troy gave me to study for the classes. I couldn't wait to tell my grandparents. I knew that their one wish was that all their grandchildren receive all the basic Catholic classes required to receive communion.

Within two weeks I started my classes at St. Mary's. The classes were very easy. I could complete all the required courses prescribed by the church in six weeks. At the end of the last class, Fr Troy gave me a handful of invitations.

"Give these to all the folks you want to invite to your big day, Joey."

"Can I fill them out now?"

"Sure, but don't you want your mom to help you?"

"No, I can do it. Do you have a phone book?"

"I most certainly do young man. I am so proud of you," Fr Troy remarked as he handed me the phone book. I noticed the invitations had envelopes with stamps already on them. That was a relief. I didn't want to ask Mom for anything. The less I bothered her, the better off I was. It had taken me years to figure that out. I eagerly filled out the invitations for my grandparents, Grace, Dad, and Jeff. "Okay, Fr Troy, I am going to walk home. Do you know where I can mail these?"

"I am going to the Post Office in the morning. I will take care of it for you." 'Okay. Thanks! See you later." As I walked home, I thought about all the people I invited. I wanted them to be a part of this most important day.

When I arrived home, I walked into a real mess. Mom was passed out drunk on the couch. She had a beer in one hand and a lit cigarette in the other. I carefully took the cigarette out of her hand and disposed of it in the ashtray. It was 8:00 p.m., and none of my brothers were around. I walked upstairs to see if they were in their bedrooms. To my relief, they were all fast asleep. I went back downstairs to help Mom to bed. As I grabbed the half-full beer from her hand, she woke up. BLAM! She hit me with her haymaker. I staggered backwards. She stood to her not-so-steady feet.

"Where the hell have you been, loser?" 'You know I have religious class every Monday night. It's been this way for the last six weeks."

"Well, those classes can't help 'stupid.' You are such a moron! Why don't you live with him? You work out with him every day. If he is such a great friend, live with him!"

"No, this is where my brothers are. Don't worry, I will be out of here in a short time." She charged toward me sticking her finger in my face."

"Well, moron, when you get kicked out of boot camp, you can't come back here!"

"What do you mean?"

"You won't pass boot camp. You don't have what it takes. Just remember once you leave you can't come back here."

She walked away from me and into the kitchen. I began to walk to the basement when I felt something hit the back of my head. I turned around to see what it was. It was the ashtray.

"What is your problem? Why do you hate me so much?" I felt the back of my head. I could feel the blood running down my neck. I looked down at my hand. My fingers were covered in blood. This was too much. I began to cry. Not because I was hurt. It's because I was trying to make something out of my life. At every turn, she had done something to hurt me.

She was standing there with a fresh alcoholic beverage in her nicotine-stained hand.

"I am going to bed."

"Yeah, you do that, idiot!" I began to walk down the stairs. I remembered I had an invitation for my ceremony. I walked back upstairs. She had retreated to the living room.

"This is for you. It's my ceremony at St. Mary's." I was standing in front of her, trying to hand her the paper. She wouldn't take it. Growing impatient, I said, "I will put this by your purse. I want you and the boys to be there."

44
MISSION ACCOMPLISHED

The day finally arrived for me to officially receive communion. For the life of me, I had no clue where Mom and the boys were. She knew about today. Even Dad was not here. I was used to that. He had been absent the majority of my life. My grandparents were here. I had gone through this process for them. I loved them so much.

I greeted my grandparents as they entered at the back of the church. Grandpa was wearing a nice grey suit. I had never seen him dressed up like that before. I gave him a big bear hug.

"I love you, Grandpa! You look very handsome."

"Thanks, Joey," he said with a big smile. As I turn to greet Grandma, I was stunned. She was wearing a beautiful red dress.

"Hi, Grandma! Thanks for coming!"

"Joey, we love you. We are so very proud of you. Did you have any doubt that we would be here?"

"No, not at all. You have always been there for me." As we made small talk, Fr Troy approached. He was wearing a flowing, gold-and-white robe. I had seen him in similar attire during Sunday Mass. From the onset of this process, I was required to attend weekly Mass. It was much different than what I was used to. However, I stayed the course because I saw the big picture. The attire Fr Troy was wearing this evening looked brand new. I guess it was worn for occasions like this.

"Okay, Joey, I need you to come with me." Fr Troy proceeded to lead me to the front of the church at which time the ceremony began. I was quite nervous as this was really going to happen. I looked in the direction of my grandparents. They were sitting in the first pew. Fr Troy began to speak into a microphone a series of questions. He led me to different stations in the church to complete the ceremony. As quickly as it began, it was over. Grandma came up to me with huge tears in her eyes.

"Honey, I have this necklace for you. It is a necklace of St. Anthony."

"Thank you! I will never take this off. As the three of us began to exit the church, Grandpa said.

"We have a surprise for you. Your Aunt Grace is having a pizza party for you."

"Really? Why?"

"Joey, I know you are hurt that your mom and brothers are not here. Grace would have been here, but she has been decorating her house for you. She loves you, Joey.

"I began to cry. I was disappointed that Grace and her crew were not here. Now I know why. They were busy decorating the house in my honor. I was so honored and touched.

Now loaded in Grandma's car, we drove over to Grace's. I was so nervous. I didn't know why; I just was. I ran as fast as I could to Grace's front door, leaving my Grandparents in my wake. Paula greeted me at the front door before I could knock.

"Joey! Congratulations! We are so proud of you!"

"Thank you, Paula,"

"Well, come on. Everyone is on the deck, waiting for you." She led me through the kitchen and outside onto the deck. Grace jumped up. She was drinking a beer visiting with Jeff, Hank, and her girls.

"Come here, Joey! Give your aunt a hug!" I ran up to Grace and hugged her as hard as I could. After our embrace, I walked over to Hank. He gave me a firm handshake from his chair. I continued to walk around, thanking everyone for their love and support. My grandparents had joined us on the deck just in time for pizza. Grace led us into the kitchen. She had Happy Joe's pizzas lined up on the counter as well as a variety of sodas.

"I have never seen so much pizza!" I said in astonishment.

"This all is for you, honey. Grab a plate and dig in."

With my food in hand, I made my way back out to the deck when Jeff said, "Joey, I am so proud of you. Where are your mom and the boys?"

"I don't know. Right now, I just want to enjoy your company. How have you been?"

"I have been fine; thanks for asking." After everyone finished eating, Stacy came out to the deck.

"Okay, everyone to the living room for cake and ice cream." *You don't have to tell me twice*, I thought. As I made my way to the living room, I saw my dad talking to Hank.

"Dad, how long have you been here?"

"I just arrived. I am sorry I was not at the church."

"That's okay! You are here now; that is all I care about," I said. He stood up from his chair to give me a handshake.

"I want a hug, Dad."

"Okay, son" As we hugged, I could smell the familiar scent of his aftershave. This smell has been etched in my mind for years. After we all enjoyed cake and ice cream, Jeff pulled me into the kitchen.

"I am heading out. Do you need a ride?"

"Yes, please"

"Okay, go say goodbye to everyone."

I made my way around the house thanking everyone for the wonderful day. I then followed Jeff to his car. He turned on some classic rock-n-roll music as we headed home. Once at the apartment, I thanked Jeff for the ride and walked into the apartment. I was so tired. It had been an awesome day. I was just hoping Mom does not ruin it when I entered the apartment.

Mom was fast asleep on the couch. I went into the kitchen to get a drink of water. As I walked by the garbage can, I saw something that caught my eye. I stared down inside the can. Sitting right on top was the invitation I gave Mom torn into a million pieces. The floodgates open as I retrieved it. I didn't want to believe what I saw. Why? Why was she so evil? I was weeping openly. The noise of my wails must have awakened her. I could hear her moving around on the couch. I bite my lip and rushed to my room. I didn't want to give her the satisfaction. That was what she wanted. I climbed into the bed and cried myself to sleep.

45
END IN SIGHT

High school was going extremely well. There were only a few weeks left before I graduated and depart for the Navy. I went to the YMCA six days a week. Five of those days were with Fr Troy and one with the boys. When I was not weight lifting, I was jogging on the streets of Dubuque. It was during these times, I could really think about things and meditate on the positive things in my life.

Mom starting dating Johnny. He was a tall, overweight black man with nothing really going for him from what I could tell. He had a Trans Am and of course the four younger boys gravitated toward that aspect. On a few occasions, he offered to take the boys for a ride in his fast car. He invited me as well, but I was not interested. I knew he was just using my mom. He picked Mom up a couple times a week up for an "AA" meeting, only to bring her home hours later, pissy drunk. On those occasions, he literally carried her into the house and plopped her on the couch. Then off he went, leaving me to deal with her. It was almost like.

"I got what I wanted from her. Now she is your problem." So here she was, in all of her glory, mean as hell!

She would lash out at anyone and everyone within reach. My brothers were not dumb. They knew it's their queue to go to their bedrooms. I felt compelled to babysit her. I was so worried she would stagger to the bar across the street—or worse—try to walk to Lynn's. The thing that scared me the most about that was that

she would get hit by a car. I turned the TV on for her. I wanted
to ensure she didn't do something stupid. However, I didn't want
to deal with her lashing out at me. I decided to go and sit on the
basement stairs. That way she didn't see me. I could hear her as
she stumbled up to her bedroom. Thank God! I sneaked upstairs a
short time later to check on her. She was passed out drunk on her
bed. Now I could go to sleep.

That pattern continued for weeks. On top of everything else,
she still blamed me for the situation with the family. It was always
the same refrain: "That ape Tyrone tried to kill me. It is because of
you! My jaw was broken! He smashed my collarbone because you
were living under the same roof as him!" She went on and on. Then
she would go into a crying rant, hollering, "I am a good mother." I
thought she was convincing herself of that but I didn't know who
believed that. As for me, she was not a mother at all. Toots was the
closest thing to a mother that we had, and now she was gone. She
was the smart one, but I was soon to follow.

For years, Mom had expected me to be a 'father figure' to my
brothers. I never could figure that out. She brought in Mark for
Marty and Greg, but that blew up in her face. Mark was heavy
handed with my brothers and soon he was out of the picture too.
We had few good male role models. Jeff was by far the greatest
influence for us boys. He accepted Leon and Andre as his nephews.
He was single with no children. Over the last few months, he had
on occasion hired us boys to clean his apartment. I thought he was
so lonely that spending time with us was a form of therapy for him.
My brothers and I cherished Jeff. He was more of a father than both
my father and stepdad combined. I knew he was excited about me
joining the Navy and getting away from the crazy family life.

No matter what was going on in his life, he always made time
for us. He was respectful toward Mom, although he did not approve
of her lifestyle. He said as much. He never talked bad about Dad,
either. He did educate us about the dangers of drinking alcohol
and its ramifications. I saw that every day. The fact that he was
investing in our lives like he was spoke for itself. I knew he tried to
help Dad with legal advice, and he had tried to get Dad to apply for

some type of assistance in order to help us out, but he was always too concerned about where his next drink was coming from.

On one occasion when I returned home from school, I found Mom passed out drunk on the living room floor and my cousin Cathy passed out on Mom's bed totally naked.

As I attempted to cover Cathy with a blanket, Mom punched me in the back of the head. Instead of taking yet another beating for no reason, I turned around and grabbed her wrist and pushed her away from me. The look on her face was something I had never seen before. She had the look like "Who do you think you are grabbing me?" She proceeded to attack me once again. I put her in a bear hug "Ma, stop! Why are you attacking me? What have I ever done to you?"

"I hate you. You are the reason I lost everything. Let me go!"

"No, I am not letting you go until you settle down!" All the commotion woke Cathy up. Here she was butt naked, trying to get Mom to settle down. Within a few moments, she convinced Mom to go to the kitchen for some coffee.

"Okay," she said through her sobs. As she was being led into the kitchen, Cathy looked back at me and mouthed the words: "This is your chance to get out of here!"

I bolted out through the front door. I sat on the front stoop for a few minutes overwhelmed with emotion. Through my pain, I decided to go for a run. The further I ran I better I felt. I discovered some time ago that by jogging, I could relieve stress. That started a routine. I would go jogging almost every day just to get away and to process everything.

We have been in Dubuque for four and a half months now. One thing was very clear to me. Dad and Mom were nothing more than two alcoholics, leaving destruction in their wake. Dad lived in the Rescue Mission. For years, all I wanted was nothing more than to be reunited with him. Now that I was older, I saw that he and Mom will never be together again. I hoped he would man up and be there for Marty and Greg. He usually came by on Sundays. He would join me and Marty as we watched our beloved Chicago Bears. It was the highlight of my week. He brought snacks to give the boys. I knew they enjoyed his company as well. He was such a good man when he was sober. It was during these times I began to understand more about my dad and what he had been doing with his life. He was never bashful when it came to his hobo lifestyle. He had shared with us during our Sunday visits about how he would travel the country via freight train, not as a passenger but as a vagabond. That was all overwhelming to me. Why didn't he stay with his family here year-round? For that matter, why didn't he stay in Rockford to be close to us?

46
THE WALLS COME TUMBLING DOWN

After a Bears victory, Dad asked, "Can you give me a haircut?"
"Dad, I don't know how to cut hair"

"You can do it I have faith in you." He was looking bushy. He certainly needed a haircut.

"Dad why don't you find a barber? I am just afraid I will screw up."

"I don't have money for that."

"Okay, I will cut your hair. Go to the kitchen." Once dad was sitting in the chair I grabbed a comb and a pair of household scissors.

"Don't move around, Dad. If you do, I may screw up your haircut."

"Okay, son," he said. I didn't know what I was doing. By the time, I got done it looked like I put a bowl on his head and cut around it. It was awful. I held my breath as I handed him a mirror.

"Oh," he said, "Thanks, Joey."

"Sorry, dad, I tried."

"It's okay. I do need to get to the mission for dinner. Do you want to go?"

"No, I have things to do here." I didn't know what he really thought of the haircut. I watched him as he exited and walked up the street. He kept running his hand through his hair. I really hoped he was not mad.

I got the answer the next day when I saw Dad staggering down the street. He was coming toward the apartment. I ran into the apartment to find my brothers. They were all upstairs playing a game.

"Hey, you guys don't come downstairs. Dad is here, and he is drunk. I don't want him around you guys. As I returned downstairs there was a loud rapping on the door. I answered the door to let him in. I could smell the awful stench of booze on his breath "Dad, why are you drinking?"

"I want to see Marty and Greg," he managed to mumble.

"They are not here. You need to leave. I don't want you to be around when you are drunk!"

"Okay, let me take a leak, and then I will leave."

"Okay." He staggered to the bathroom. I couldn't let him leave like this. I needed to do something. I will walk him to the mission. When he returned to the front door I could tell he was mad about something.

"Dad, I want to walk you to the Mission."

"You don't need to. I will be fine"

"Dad, you are not fine! I am concerned that you will get hit by a car, fall and hit your head, or get arrested. Let me help you, please!"

"You have done enough already. I can't go anywhere in public without a hat. You butchered my hair. Thanks a lot!"

"I told you I don't know how to cut hair. You insisted I do it, so deal with it! Bye, be safe" I replied as I closed the door behind him. There was nothing else I could do Not only have I had to deal with Mom and Tyrone for years, now it was him. It was just too much! The fact was, all four boys were home, but I did not want them to see him in that condition. I had no regrets.

Mom returned home with Johnny just minutes after Dad left. Thank God, she did not see him in that condition. She loved to tear into him at every turn. To my surprise, she was sober. Johnny was sober as well. I was upset with the exchange with Dad. I knew I couldn't discuss how I felt with Mom. Seemed like a good time to go for a run. Maybe Grace will be home. We have had so many good talks. I could use her insight about Dad. I was at my wits end with him. Mom and Johnny were in the kitchen now. She was in a good mood for a change. The boys must have heard her come home. They all ran down the stairs and into the kitchen. They were all take turns hugging her. It was almost as if she had been away for years. I walked into the kitchen. When I saw my chance, I asked.

"Mom, do you mind if I go for a run? I want to pay Grace a visit."

"Why do you have anything to do with her? I am still upset that she never helped us move here the first time!"

"She is a great woman and my favorite aunt."

"I don't care. Just get out of my face!" As I walked away from her, I glanced over at Johnny. He looked at me as if to say, "Get lost, kid!"

As I began to jog over to her place, I was mindful that she was close to Dad. She always was the point person in the family who could find him anywhere. In past summers when I could come to town, she always got a hold of him somehow some way. For that I will always be grateful. The relationship with his brothers had been strained for years. I didn't know if it's because of the drinking or a combination of things—especially the relationship with Frank. Whenever they were together, an argument would ensue.

Once I arrived at Grace's place, she greeted me with her huge smile.

"Hi, Joey, come in, honey," she said through the open kitchen door. I opened the screen door and walked in. She was sitting at the kitchen table, talking on the phone.

"Mom, Joey is here. I need to go, bye." I visited with Grace once a week or so. I didn't waste any time telling her about Dad showing up drunk.

"Grace, I don't understand why Dad has lived the life of a hobo."

"Joey, do you believe your Dad left you kids when you were very young because he wanted to? Do you believe it is his entire fault?"

"No, of course not, but I don't understand why he was never around if he loves us."

"You are old enough now to know some things about your dad. When he was born, there was a hole in his skull. He almost died as a result. This affected his brain, and as a result he had struggles like you can never imagine. When he was thirteen, he was riding his bike when a truck hit him. He suffered a major skull fracture. This injury almost cost him his life as well. So, you see, honey, your dad was dealt a bad hand from the very beginning. He struggled as a teenager to the point that he was sent away to Eldora. It's a juvenile jail. Furthermore, your mom was having an affair with Tyrone. He would go to work out the front door, and Tyrone would come in the back door. And as far as him not wanting to see you kids, he would call me countless times while in Rockford. He made many attempts to see you kids. Tyrone would not allow him to come around. Your dad moved out, knowing what was going on. He didn't have the skills necessary to deal with this. You need to know the truth Joey! Your dad loves all of you kids! I know that for a fact! So, I hope as you prepare for this new chapter in your life, you can do so on a clean slate with your dad."

I was beginning to understand more about Dad.. I began to wail uncontrollably. Grace walked over to the counter and grabbed some tissue.

"Here, honey, I am sorry to be the one to tell you all of this." Grace excused herself from the kitchen. When she returned, she handed me a book. She had it opened to a picture of a group of men in a group. As I looked up at her, she had tears running down her face. Her voice broke with emotion.

"Joey, here are a bunch of pictures of your dad at the rescue mission in Denver." I studied the photos as Grace continued: "I know it makes you sad to hear your dad is a hobo, a drifter. He is at his happiest when he is riding the rails all over the place. He often told me he felt free as a bird. I want you to look at all the photos of your dad in that book. He is smiling ear to ear because he was content. In fact, he has many fond memories of all the people he met and the places he visited."

Armed with what Grace had shared with me and seeing the photos of him, all I could say was, "I didn't know. I didn't know." Grace walked over to try to console me.

"I now understand, Aunt Grace, and I love him now more than ever! Whatever unforgiveness and resentment I had is now gone. Thank you!"

"You deserve to know, and I am glad I am the one who was able to explain your dad" I glanced at the clock—8:00 p.m.

"Oh boy, it's late. I need to get home, Aunt Grace,"

"Okay, Joey, bye. I love you!" With that, I ran home as fast as I could, I felt like a million pounds were lifted off my chest. I couldn't wait to see Dad again. I wanted to tell him that I had forgiven him for everything and that I knew in my heart that everything was not his fault, contrary to what Mom and my stepdad programmed us all to believe.

47
SHORT TIMER

I completed high school on January 11, the day after my birthday. There was no birthday celebration. I became more restless over the next ten days. I wanted to close this chapter of my life on a good note and launch headlong into my military career. I dread being out of school and waiting around the house because I really didn't want to be around her more than I had. I've taken more than enough abuse from her throughout the years, both physically and emotionally. I was done with it. I wanted to see dad before I shipped out.

I refused to allow her to push me around and treat me like dirt. I spent as much time as I could over the next ten days with my brothers. I was really going to miss them.

I was concerned about the direction my family would go after I leave. Even though Mom had ingrained in me that I was a piece of garbage and that I would never be anything, I knew better. And although she never apologized for the way she treated me over the years, I still loved her.

I would prove to her and to anyone else who had doubts that I would be successful in the next chapter of my life. It was motivation that drove me. Mom had reminded me daily that I would never get through boot camp. She would also say I would never succeed in life. I would be just like my dad, according to her She was anything but a positive source of inspiration over the years.

Underway

The day had finally arrived for me to ship out. I was sad that.Dad had not been around. He knew I was leaving. Where could he be? I had packed a small gym bag with just the bare items that I would need. That morning I spent extra time with the boys around the breakfast table. I told them how much I loved them. I gave each one a very long embrace as they departed for school.

Mom was avoiding me as usual. She was in the kitchen slipping her instant coffee. She was writing a letter to somebody. God only knows who. I needed to get outside to catch the city bus. It will be here any moment. I put on my coat, hat, and gloves and walked back into the kitchen to say goodbye. As I entered the kitchen, I said, "Mom, I love you. I'm going to miss you. Please be safe." She continued to write on the paper. She didn't even look at me. That was fine! What happened next probably surprised her when I walked out the front door. I held my head high as I walked out of the house with all the confidence in the world.

Just as I made my way to the other side of the street onto the sidewalk, Mom walked out of the apartment with just her house-coat on. She began to holler at me.

"You are never going to make it in boot camp. You are a pathetic loser. You're just a waste of space, and just remember you can never come back here to live. Good riddance, moron! Boy! I needed a boost of confidence, and I could always count on mom to deliver that day or night

The bus pulled up. I paid the fare and walked to the back of the bus. I looked back at her. Her face was contorted, waving her arms and screaming at the top of her lungs. I was embarrassed for her. More than that, I was worried about the welfare of my brothers. As the bus pulled off, I watched as she faded away in the distance.

When the dust settled I was still standing. They couldn't destroy me. They couldn't steal my joy. I had the tenacity, the determination, to move on, to never give up, to never quit. More than anything, I found forgiveness toward Dad, and still had love in my heart for my Mom even after many years of her abuse.

In all I that I went through I was never truly alone. God was there. I did not know it then but I know today that God had a plan for me.

Fear not, for I am with you;

Be not dismayed, for I am your God.

I will strengthen you,

Yes, I will help you,

I will uphold you with My righteous right hand.

(Isa. 41:10)

CPSIA information can be obtained
at www.ICGtesting.com
Printed in the USA
BVHW041803150322
631532BV00011BA/602